To someone special

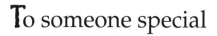

From

Date

365 Days to

Knowing God

for Girls

Carolyn Larsen

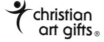
christian
art gifts ®

365 Days to Knowing God for Girls

Text copyright © 2009 by Educational Publishing Concepts.
All rights reserved.

© 2009 Christian Art Gifts, RSA
Christian Art Gifts, Inc., IL, USA

First edition 2009

Designed by Christian Art Gifts

Images used under license from Shutterstock.com

Set in 12 on 14 pt Palatino Lt Std
by Christian Art Gifts

Printed in China

ISBN 978-1-77036-148-5

09 10 11 12 13 14 15 16 17 18 – 11 10 9 8 7 6 5 4 3 2

Foreword

The kind of food you put into your body determines how healthy you are. In the same way, the kind of thoughts you put into your mind determines how well your spirit is. This book gives you a healthy way to start your day by reading a verse from God's Word and focusing your thoughts on how much He loves you. The ChallengePoint gives you an action point – something to think about all day as you learn to live for God and recognize His loving care in your life.

My prayer for you is that the topics in this book encourage you to understand how much God loves you and cares about every area of your life!

God is fond of you.
  If He had a wallet,
your photo would be in it.
  If He had a refrigerator,
your picture would be on it.
  He sends you flowers every spring
and a sunrise every morning.
  Face it, friend, He's crazy about you.
                              ~ MAX LUCADO

January

Knowing God by
His Love

How precious are Your thoughts about me, O God. They cannot be numbered!

✳ PSALM 139:17

Did you know that God thinks about you? Isn't that incredible? God, the Creator of EVERYTHING thinks about you. He doesn't just think about you once in a while or when you do something wrong. He thinks about you so often that His thoughts can't even be counted. Wow. That's a lot!

Why does God think about you so much? Simple answer … He loves you. Yep, and when you love someone, you care about what's happening in her life and you think about hanging out with her and sharing secrets and dreams. Well, God cares about you that much. He wants to know what's on your mind and He wants to know your problems, hopes, dreams and well … everything.

ChallengePoint

Maybe there are times when you don't feel God's love. During times when nothing is going right, you may wonder about His love. You may ask yourself if He even knows about your problems and your pain. Well, now you know the answer to that question. He knows. He loves you. He thinks about you all the time!

Knowing God by
Witnessing His Power

God is the one who began this good work in you, and I am certain that He won't stop before it is complete on the day that Christ Jesus returns.

✳ PHILIPPIANS 1:6

Imagine a feather floating downward, dipping and turning, falling then floating again. It doesn't travel in a straight line and there's no way to tell where it's going.

Right now you probably have hopes and dreams for what you want to be when you grow up. But as you grow up, things change and you go one way for a while, then another way. Did you miss God's plan?

Sometimes He guides you in a direction that seems like the opposite of where you thought you were headed. But God has already started working in your life – He still has a plan for you and He *will* finish it.

ChallengePoint

You have a part in this plan of God to finish what He started in your life. He will keep revealing new things to you if you will obey Him. One of the best ways to receive His guidance is to read His Word and listen for His guidance. Trust Him – He has a plan for YOU and He will keep on working on it, as long as you're on this planet.

Knowing God by
Obeying Him

"Everyone who hears these words of Mine and puts them into practice is like a wise man who built his house on the rock."

✳ MATTHEW 7:24

What's smart about building a house on solid rock? God knows you need a strong foundation to get through life – a foundation that will help you make good choices and keep you close to Him when things get tough. These words of Jesus give the true formula for who's smart and who isn't: "Listen to and obey Jesus' teachings and you're the smart one."

God wants to give you all the wisdom you need for life. But don't just read the words, listen to what they say and obey them. He wants you to put His words into action in your life. That's what makes you smart and makes a good foundation to build on for the future.

ChallengePoint

A girl who thinks she has all the answers – about EVERYTHING – likes to make everyone else feel dumb. Do you know someone who knows everything about everything (or THINKS she does)? Instead of letting her bug you, ask God to show you how to love her – that's listening to His Word (to love others) and obeying Him. THAT makes you the smart one!

Knowing God by
Showing Courage

God is our refuge and strength, an ever-present help in trouble.

✳ PSALM 46:1

The world can be a scary place sometimes. When you watch the news you see terrible things that people do to other people. You see frightening natural disasters that occur. Sometimes life gets stinky on a personal level – friends are mean, school is hard, or family is confusing. When those times come and you need a place to get away – you've got it.

God promised to be your "get-away-place." In fact, He wants to be because He loves you so much. He is standing by, ready to help you, whatever the problem.

Because you are His child, He will give you strength to get through whatever is before you. You should know that you are never alone. God is with you and will help you – always.

ChallengePoint

There will be times when you don't "feel" God's presence. That's where faith comes in. You've got His promise here, that He is always ready to help you and that He will be your strength and your hiding place. Have the courage to trust His Word, trust Him to do what He says He will do – even if you can't "feel" His presence.

Knowing God by
Praying

When I asked for Your help, You answered my prayer and gave me courage.

✳ PSALM 138:3

Some people treat God as if He is a big Santa Claus in the sky. Just ask Him whatever you want and BAM … it's yours! Sorry, but it doesn't work that way. It is true that God invites you to pray to Him and tell Him any and everything that is on your mind. He wants to know.

It's also true that He answers your prayers, just as this verse tells you. But look at the last phrase of the verse. Sometimes God answers your prayer to make another girl stop picking on you or to help someone get over an illness, not by following the "order" you give Him, but by giving you the strength to get through it.

ChallengePoint

The comfort of prayer is that God does hear your prayers – whatever you may pray for – and He does answer your prayers. However, the answer may not be really obvious to you at first. It may be obvious later, after the crisis has passed and you realize that you've made it through … because of the strength He gave you.

Knowing God by
Serving Him

"Do to others whatever you would like them to do to you. This is the essence of all that is taught in the law and prophets."

✳ M<small>ATTHEW</small> 7:12

Treat others the way you want them to treat you. Simple, huh? If you want others to be kind, gentle, forgiving, helpful, encouraging … treat them that way first. Did you get that? – FIRST. Even if they are mean, spiteful, critical, unkind and accusing – you should be nice. Wow, that's tough, isn't it?

Does this verse mean that people will automatically be nice if you are nice first? Not necessarily. So, why should you be so nice to them? Because God says you should – it's the way He wants you to treat others.

ChallengePoint

Of course you want to be treated kindly by others. If you are consistently kind and caring, it may rub off on those around you. But even if it doesn't, you'll be obeying God by living the way He teaches. That's the best thing. If others are still mean to you, let God take care of them. Just be the best that you can be!

Knowing God by
Giving

"Give, and you will receive. Your gift will return to you in full – pressed down, shaken together to make room for more, running over, and poured into your lap. The amount you give will determine the amount you get back."

✳ LUKE 6:38

Here's a fun thing to do – with your parents' permission. Get the brown sugar out and pour some into a measuring cup. Make the cup full to the top. Now, take a spoon and press the brown sugar down. Press hard. Now you can get even more sugar in, even though you thought the cup was full before.

That's how God's blessings come to you when you're generous to others. He keeps giving and giving, even when you think it isn't possible for Him to give more. Oh, God may not give you "stuff." His gifts are often more inside gifts such as peace and joy and the knowledge that you are obeying Him. Really, those are the best gifts.

ChallengePoint

Don't think this verse means that if you give you will get more money or stuff in return. God looks at your heart and the reason you're giving in the first place. Giving in order to get is the wrong reason to give, so don't expect anything in return. Give because you love God and want to obey Him.

"You will search for Me. And when you search for Me with all your heart, you will find Me."

✳ JEREMIAH 29:13

Have you ever lost something that was really important to you? Something you really cared about? Did you just kind of stand and look around and if you didn't see it just say, "Oh well"? Or did you get down on your hands and knees and look under things, through piles of things, and literally turn the room upside down looking for this thing?

Yeah, that's looking with all your heart. God shouldn't be someone you can take or leave. Maybe you think, "Well, if I'm close to God today fine – if not, that's fine too." Feeling that way means you don't really care and you probably won't connect with Him at all then.

ChallengePoint

God wants to be NUMBER ONE in your heart. He loves you more than anything and He wants you to love Him right back. So, if you're kind of wimpy about spending time with Him or reading your Bible you will not have a close relationship with God. Don't expect Him to do all the work!

Knowing God by
Enduring

I run with purpose in every step. I am not just shadowboxing. I discipline my body like an athlete, training it to do what it should. Otherwise, I fear that after preaching to others I myself might be disqualified.

✳ 1 CORINTHIANS 9:26-27

When something is worth doing, it is worth doing well. That means it's going to take work and sometimes that work will be hard. Don't give up just because it's hard though. Be willing to work hard.

You have to set your mind on the goal of finishing strong and not letting anything keep you from reaching your goal.

The process of learning how to live in this world is a goal to set before your heart. Keeping that focus as your finish line gives you a goal to strive for.

ChallengePoint

The Bible says that the greatest commandment is to love God with all your heart, soul and mind and the second commandment is to love others as you love yourself. Love like that shows that you are God's child. Don't just *talk* about loving like that ... *do it*. That's a goal to put all your energy and strength toward. You'll be learning to live like Jesus and be the kind of girl God wants you to be.

So you must stop telling lies. Tell each other the truth, because we all belong to each other in the same body.

✳ EPHESIANS 4:25

Once you start lying, it's very tough to stop. It starts simply – with one little "white" lie. Then you have to tell another one in order to protect the first one. Then, another and another. Pretty soon it's hard to remember what's true and what's a lie.

Why do you tell lies? Usually to keep yourself out of trouble or to make yourself look good to other people. It feels lousy to be lied to so it only makes sense that your lies make others feel lousy too.

Jesus didn't lie to people. He told the truth, even when it was hard to hear or when it put Him in danger. Truthfulness makes you more like Jesus. It's the right way to treat others.

ChallengePoint

God expects you to be truthful. His Word says that you should love other people as much as you love yourself. Lying is not loving. Honesty is loving. The goal in your Christian life is to honestly become more and more like Jesus. Begin with honesty wrapped in kindness and love.

Knowing God by
Praying

Give all your worries to Him, because He cares about you.

* 1 PETER 5:7

Prayer is an amazing privilege. Think about it – you can talk to the God who created everything! What's even more amazing is that God loves you. He proves it over and over every day.

Since God loves you that much, it only makes sense that He wants to know what's going on in your life. He cares about all the things that worry you. So, tell Him what's on your mind. Tell Him everything.

There is nothing you can tell God that will shock or surprise Him. In fact, He knows what you're thinking and feeling anyway, so be honest with Him. Tell Him and ask Him to take care of your problems.

ChallengePoint

God loves you so much. Since He does, He wants to take care of you and protect you. He wants to know what you're afraid of; what you worry about; what you celebrate. The cool thing is you can give all your worries to God. He will take care of them. You can trust Him to do that because He loves you!

Knowing God by
Trusting Him

The LORD gives perfect peace to those whose faith is firm.

✳ ISAIAH 26:3

Peace is something everyone wants to have. But a quick look around our world will show you that very few people actually have it; countries are at war, gangs battle in cities, families fight with one another, and people are just downright mean to others.

What does it take to have personal peace that will flow out to those around you? Simple answer: Faith in God. Firm faith in God. That means that you trust Him with everything in your life. You know He will take care of you. He will guide you. He will protect you from people who want to hurt you.

ChallengePoint

Trusting God means that you know He has a plan for your life and that you can trust that plan completely. There is nothing for you to worry about. You can trust God completely when you have a strong, steady faith. Your trust in Him doesn't waffle back and forth depending on whether things are going well. You trust Him because you know He loves you and wants the best for you. That brings peace.

Knowing God by
Using His Gifts

The sun has one kind of glory, while the moon and stars each have another kind. And even the stars differ from each other in their glory.

✳ 1 CORINTHIANS 15:41

You are unique. God made you just the way He wants you to be, with special talents and abilities. There may be times when you don't feel special as you look around and see other girls with talents you wish were yours.

It's tempting to compare yourself to others when you hear someone with a beautiful singing voice, great athletic ability, or great intelligence. Maybe you look at yourself and don't see anything special. But remember that God made every person different and gave each one the abilities they would need to do the special job He has for them.

ChallengePoint

Every star is different from the others and the sun and moon have different jobs, yet each one is necessary and important to life on this planet. The lesson to learn is: Don't compare yourself to someone else, instead look for the special interests and abilities God gave you and get busy searching for how to use those for His work. Think how boring the world would be if God had made all people exactly alike!

Seeking His Protection

I will lie down and sleep in peace, for You alone, O LORD, make me dwell in safety.

* PSALM 4:8

Spooky sounds in your dark room … Strange shadows floating across the walls … Imagination running wild. Do these kinds of things ever keep you up at night? Why do you stay awake with your breath coming in short gasps? Because you are afraid. You don't feel safe. Something is frightening you.

However, when you trust God's love for you, you can sleep like a baby. You can know that He is on guard, watching out for you and protecting you. He loves you more than you can imagine. God will take care of you and nothing can stand against Him. His power is awesome. You are safe.

ChallengePoint

When you're having one of those nights when you're scared – even if you don't know why – and you just can't sleep, remember Psalm 4:8. It's a reminder that God is on guard watching out for you. He's patrolling around you all the time; protecting you. You don't have to worry about anything because He loves you completely and is keeping you safe.

Knowing God by
His Forgiveness

"Come now, let's settle this," says the LORD. "Though your sins are like scarlet, I will make them as white as snow. Though they are red like crimson, I will make them as white as wool."

✳ ISAIAH 1:18

Everyone thinks they deserve forgiveness – even if they do not easily give it to others. The model of true forgiveness is God Himself. God is perfect. He never does anything wrong. You, on the other hand, cannot help doing some wrong things because, as the Bible says, everyone sins. God doesn't have to forgive you for your sins, but He does. He forgives you and forgets the sins – you are clean and faultless in His eyes. That happens because Jesus came to earth and died for your sins.

When you ask Jesus into your heart, confess your sins and ask forgiveness for them, God wipes them out. They're gone. That's true forgiveness!

ChallengePoint

Do you say you forgive, but throw it back in the person's face the next time you get mad? God doesn't do that. When He forgives you, He cleanses you – He washes away the dirt. His forgiveness is complete because of Christ's sacrifice. Let Him be your model for forgiveness for others. Forgive and forget.

Seeking His Guidance

"For I know the plans I have for you," declares the LORD, "plans to prosper you and not to harm you, plans to give you hope and a future."

✳ JEREMIAH 29:11

You're only a kid so you don't have to know the plans for your whole life. But do you wonder what your life will be like in 10 or 15 years' time? Will you be in some boring job that you hate getting up for each day?

There's a way to know that your future will be everything you hope for … seek God's guidance. He has a plan for you that began before you were even born. His plans for you are good. He loves you so much that He wants the best for you. His plans will make you an amazing woman.

ChallengePoint

God *does* have a plan for your life. He wants good things for you. But those good things may not include money or fame. God cares more about what is happening in your heart. He wants you to learn to be a better person who lives for Him, trusts Him and loves Him. That's what His plan involves. So, to be the best you can possibly be, seek God's guidance. Find out what His plan is for your life.

Knowing God by
Understanding Anger

In your anger do not sin: Do not let the sun go down while you are still angry.

* EPHESIANS 4:26

Think about a time when you were really mad at someone. Grrrr! Did you just want to shout about how mad you were? Sometimes it's hard to get over being angry, especially if the person who hurt you isn't even sorry.

Some people get so mad that they lie in bed and plan out ways to get even and hurt the person they are mad at. That's not good and definitely doesn't please God.

God tells people to love one another. Revenge and love don't go together. Notice, God doesn't say not to get angry. He knows people will get angry once in a while. He says that when you do get angry you should handle it in the right way ... don't sin.

ChallengePoint

Go to the person you are angry with and talk with her right away. Try very hard to settle the problem and keep your friendship strong. Don't waste your energy by plotting out revenge or losing sleep over it. Remember to show God's love to others by settling your problems quickly. Don't let friendships be broken by anger.

Great is His faithfulness; His mercies begin afresh each morning.
* LAMENTATIONS 3:23

It's impossible to be 100% obedient and faithful to God, because human beings are sinful creatures. You do wrong things sometimes, even if you don't mean to. The cool thing is that God never stops loving you! He doesn't get tired of taking care of you and loving you.

It doesn't matter how often you fail to love Him back and obey Him, God will keep on loving you and taking care of you. Every day is a new experience of receiving His love and care.

ChallengePoint

God doesn't store up complaints against you and then one day just say, "I'm through with you!" His love never gives up on you! Every day with God is a new experience of His complete love and care. He loves giving gifts to you. Always remember how much He loves you and begin every day by telling Him that you love Him too. Ask His forgiveness for the times you disobeyed Him, and ask Him to help you be stronger in living for Him each day.

Knowing God by
Seeking Salvation

Jesus answered, "I am the way and the truth and the life. No one comes to the Father except through Me."

✳ JOHN 14:6

God's Word tells you that His wish is for everyone – all people – to accept Jesus as Savior and be with God in heaven someday. He wants everyone to know that their "forever" will be in heaven. But people can't just walk into heaven, because every person sins and no sin is allowed in heaven. That's why God made a plan of salvation that saves people from their sin and makes them clean enough to come to heaven with Him.

Some people might say that there are several ways to get into heaven, but that's not what the Bible says. God's Word teaches that there is one way, and only one way, to be saved.

❊ ChallengePoint

✳ Jesus is the only doorway to heaven. What does that mean? Simple. When you accept Jesus into your heart as your Savior, confess your sins and ask His forgiveness, then you are saved. You can plan on going to heaven someday. There is no other way; no shortcut; nothing simpler. Jesus is the only way.

Sing praises to the LORD; praise our God with harps.

* PSALM 147:7

A lot of people sing when they are really, really happy. They may not sing well, but joy just kind of flows out of them because they are so happy.

God would like your thanks to Him to come from that same kind of joyful heart. He gives you so many wonderful things each day. He protects you, guides you and loves you incredibly! Let thankfulness fly out of your heart on wings of joy and happiness.

ChallengePoint

There are stories in the Bible of times when Jesus did wonderful miracles for people but they forgot to thank Him. Those stories are a reminder of how important it is to say "thank You." It's easy for prayers to get filled up with asking God to "Do this" or "Give me that," instead of just a simple "Thanks for all You do for me." Take time to notice all God does for you each day and you will begin to understand how very much He loves you. Then, take time to thank Him each day.

Knowing God by
Celebrating Him

Let everything that breathes praise the LORD. Praise the LORD!
* PSALM 150:6

What do you have to do to celebrate something? You must know, enjoy and appreciate it. To celebrate God means getting to know Him through reading His Word, spending time with Him and talking with Him. You can't celebrate who God is unless you know something about Him. As you begin understanding facts such as His total love for you that caused Him to send His only Son to earth, and the sacrifice of Jesus to die for your sins when He Himself was sinless; you can't help but celebrate God.

It's easy to take for granted things that you've heard all your life – God's love – Jesus' life – Jesus' death and resurrection. But treating them as something worth celebrating changes your view of God's awesome love and power.

ChallengePoint

Don't "get used" to the idea that God loves you. Celebrate it! Think of ways to remind yourself how incredible it is that the Creator of the universe knows your name, loves you and cares for you.

Loving Others

"But I say to you, love your enemies. Pray for those who hurt you. If you do this, you will be true children of your Father in heaven. He causes the sun to rise on good people and on evil people, and He sends rain to those who do right and to those who do wrong."

✳ MATTHEW 5:44-45

Does God really want you to be nice to people who are mean to you? Yeah, He does. He even wants you to pray for them … pray NICE things, not stuff like "make her spill soda all over her desk in front of the whole class." The thing that makes God's children different from those who don't know Him is … love. Yep. You see, God does good things for both good people and bad people because He loves all people.

When you're acting like your Father, you will be nice to all people too – even those who aren't nice to you. You'll even pray for good things to happen to those who hurt you … that's showing a family likeness to your Father.

ChallengePoint

God's goal for your life is that you become more and more like Him. That means He wants you to love all people, just as He does. God is defined by love. 1 John 4:16 says, "God is love." So, becoming like God means learning to love all people.

Knowing God by
Suppressing My Pride

You save the humble, but You bring down those who are proud.
* PSALM 18:27

Neener neener, boo, boo, I am the coolest!" Proud people are all about themselves. Yeah, a bragger sings her own praises and tries to convince the world that she is the most awesome thing since sliced bread.

A person consumed with pride can't let herself praise anyone else. She won't recognize anyone else's successes or victories because she always has to be the best.

This is not pleasant. More important than not being pleasant, it's not pleasing to God. He's not a fan of braggers, in fact, He will bring down a proud person.

ChallengePoint

So God isn't a fan of pride ... so God is a fan of humility ... so what? So, stop being proud. Duh. Stop bragging about yourself. Don't be a person who always has to be the winner or the best. Let someone else win and when she wins, become her biggest cheerleader. That's the way God wants you to live. It will please Him.

Abiding in Him

Come close to God, and God will come close to you. Wash your hands, you sinners; purify your hearts, for your loyalty is divided between God and the world.

✴ JAMES 4:8

Abiding is one of those words that isn't often used in normal conversation. When you're abiding it means you are sticking close, like super-strong glue that holds things together so tightly that they can't come apart. However, if the two objects do get separated you can see little bits of one piece stuck on the other one.

Abiding in God means sticking really close to Him. God wants to be so close to you that you can't be pulled apart – but if you do separate from Him, there will still be evidence of Him that sticks with you.

ChallengePoint

Abiding means hanging on tight to God. Staying close, no matter what pops up in your life. It isn't always easy, but it's the best way to get to know God. You know that the more time you spend with someone, the better you get to know her. So, sticking close to God means you get to know Him better and better. That's exactly what He wants for you. Cool, huh?

Knowing God by
Trusting Him

"Come to Me, all of you who are tired and have heavy loads, and I will give you rest."

✳ MATTHEW 11:28

Jesus loves you … a lot. This Scripture verse proves it. He loves you so much that He wants to help you with stuff that gets you down. He knows that life gets tough once in a while.

Since you're a kid, it may be that you get overloaded with homework and chores; or maybe it's friend troubles; maybe really serious stuff like someone you love being really sick is what gets you down. Whatever it is, Jesus offers to help.

ChallengePoint

Will you go to Jesus for help with your problems? Maybe you think, "How will God help me with the kind of problems I have?" He will help in ways you may not even have thought of. First, He will remind you that you aren't alone. He's with you no matter what you're going through. He may answer prayers to change situations. He will bring people around you who will encourage you and support you. He will also give you strength to get through whatever life brings. He loves you … come to Him.

Knowing God by
Using His Gifts

Don't be concerned about the outward beauty of fancy hairstyles, expensive jewelry, or beautiful clothes. You should clothe yourselves instead with the beauty that comes from within, the unfading beauty of a gentle and quiet spirit, which is so precious to God.

* 1 PETER 3:3-4

Time to be honest … figure out how much time you spend on your appearance. That includes shopping for clothes, working on your hair, looking at magazines or websites about clothes and hair, thinking about those things or looking at what famous people wear or how their hair looks.

OK, now compare that amount of time with how much time you spend thinking about living for God, learning how to be like Him, talking with Him, telling others about Him. Which amount is more? Yeah, surprising, isn't it?

ChallengePoint

The interesting thing is that what matters most to God is not how you look on the outside. He cares more about how you look on the inside – what condition your heart is in. The more you learn to be like Him and live in a way that reflects His love and spirit to others, the more beautiful you are to Him. Rather than having the latest styles, God would prefer to see old-fashioned gentleness and kindness in your heart.

Knowing God by
His Love

The LORD is compassionate and gracious, slow to anger, abounding in love.

✻ PSALM 103:8

God doesn't just *say* that He loves you – He shows it. He cares when you're hurting or sad. In fact, He wants to help you by being your comfort. He wants you to tell Him when you're sad, scared, or whatever. He shows His love by giving you … well, everything you have. He gives out of His kindness and love. And He forgives when you mess up.

Unlike some people, God doesn't get angry quickly. He keeps giving you more chances to get things right. That may be one of the best parts of His love for you, it takes Him a LONG time to get angry. Close your eyes and imagine the tons of water flowing over Niagara Falls – God loves you more than that. Imagine the zillion stars in the sky – He loves you more than that! God's love just keeps on coming and coming.

ChallengePoint

In God's world, love is a verb – it is action. So what, you ask? So, acknowledge and accept His love. Thank Him for it … and then pass it along to others.

Knowing God by
Praying to Him

But whenever they were in trouble and turned to the LORD, the God of Israel, and sought Him out, they found Him.

* 2 CHRONICLES 15:4

You've probably played the game, Hide 'n Seek. Of course, the goal is to be really good at hiding so that the person who is "It" can't find you. So you look for the best hiding place and stay really quiet, hoping that you become invisible. If you can touch home base without being discovered by "It", then you win, right?

It's a fun game to play. But it's not one you can ever play with God. When you actually look for Him you will find out that He is not hiding. Nope, it's more like He's jumping in front of you and waving His arms because He wants to be found. So, why does it seem sometimes like He isn't around, especially when you're in trouble?

ChallengePoint

God doesn't force His way into your life. He wants to help you but you have to LOOK for Him. That means reading His Word, praying, and being quiet so you can hear His voice. When you do these things it shows that you're serious about wanting His help.

Knowing God by
Seeking His Protection

You are my hiding place; You will protect me from trouble; and surround me with songs of deliverance.

✳ PSALM 32:7

Did you ever wish you could be invisible for a while? Maybe when someone is unhappy with you or when you're in some kind of trouble … you'd like to be invisible so no one can find you. That would keep you safe and out of trouble, wouldn't it?

Did you know that God is willing to do that for you? He doesn't make you invisible, but He hides you, especially from Satan and his sneaky attacks.

God just kind of covers you over so Satan can't even find you. God keeps you safe and then He and His angels cheer your safety!

ChallengePoint

Wow, that's awesome, isn't it? How do you get God's protection? Just ask for it. Yep, that's it. Ask Him to protect you, and then stay as close to Him as you can by reading His Word and talking with Him. That's an important step. Show God that you seriously want His protection and you're not just going to talk to Him when you have trouble.

Serving Him

"No one can serve two masters. For you will hate one and love the other; you will be devoted to one and despise the other. You cannot serve both God and money."

✳ LUKE 16:13

It's a scientific fact that two objects cannot occupy the same space at the same time. It's impossible. So, it only makes sense that there cannot be two things that have the Number One place in your heart. It just won't work.

You have to choose whether you want to live for God by obeying Him and serving Him and learning to be like Him or if you want to serve something else. For example, if you make your friends the most important thing in your life or sports or music – anything – then God is not ruling your life. The struggle in your heart when you try to make two things the most important in your life, will make you miserable.

ChallengePoint

It's a simple choice – serve God or something else. God loves you so much and He wants all your heart. He wants you to serve Him by getting to know Him, obeying Him and telling others about Him. If you've given something else the Number One spot in your heart, maybe you should reconsider.

Knowing God by
Obeying Him

We may think we are doing the right thing, but the LORD always knows what is in our hearts.

✳ PROVERBS 21:2

Excuses, excuses, excuses. Do you have an excuse for every mistake or bad choice you make? Most people can come up with an excuse for bad behavior or bad choices and their excuses always make them look good. The problems they have are always someone else's fault.

Well, as this Scripture verse says, you can make all the excuses you want to protect your reputation but you won't be fooling God. He sees right through to your heart and what your true motives are.

ChallengePoint

So, if God sees your heart and knows why you truly behave the way you do, there is no point in making excuses. God cares more about what's in your heart than what you say. That's because what's in your heart (your motives) will eventually come through in your actions. He wants your heart to love and obey Him. When that happens, you won't have to worry about excuses because you'll live the way you should.

Within each of us, just waiting to blossom, is the wonderful promise of all we can be.

~ ANONYMOUS

February

Knowing God by
Confessing Sin

Finally, I confessed all my sins to You and stopped trying to hide my guilt. I said to myself, "I will confess my rebellion to the LORD." And You forgave me! All my guilt is gone.

* PSALM 32:5

Let's face it – if there is one thing some girls are really good at it's guilt. Yeah, for whatever reason, some girls can't get over the guilt when they've hurt someone or did something bad.

Guilt really gets in the way of your relationship with God. It's hard to be honest with Him when you're hiding things and dealing with the guilt of that. So … come clean! Just tell Him when you've had bad thoughts and done mean things. Just tell Him. And guess what … He will forgive you. So … BAM … the guilt is gone and is replaced with forgiveness!

ChallengePoint

Confessing is hard because it means you have to admit things out loud – at least out loud in prayer. But hiding things is hard too, especially from God who knows everything you do anyway. Guilt is no fun. It weighs you down and colors everything you do and feel. So, come clean – confess and accept His forgiveness.

Finally, my friends, keep your minds on whatever is true, pure, right, holy, friendly, and proper. Don't ever stop thinking about what is truly worthwhile and worthy of praise.

✳ PHILIPPIANS 4:8

So … when you "do your hair" what kind of product do you put in? Mousse or gel? What do you want the product to do? Keep it straight or make it curl? What product you use will determine the end result of your hair look. Now, if you put, say … mayonnaise in, then your hair will be kind of greasy. If you put gelatin in, it will be kind of stiff. What you put in determines the outcome.

Same thing is true of your mind. What you put in it determines what comes out in your thoughts and how you behave. It also determines whether God will be able to guide you.

ChallengePoint

Keep your thoughts on the kinds of things that show you're serious about living for God. Think about things that honor Him. If you do that, then you are much more likely to see His guidance show up in your life. He will guide your thoughts and your decisions.

Knowing God by
Understanding Anger

My dear brothers and sisters, always be willing to listen and slow to speak. Do not become angry easily, because anger will not help you live the right kind of life God wants.

✳ JAMES 1:19-20

You hear that a friend told a lie about you. The lie spreads to more people and grows in size. The next time you see that friend, you blow up and say all kinds of ugly things to her. When you finally walk away, she KNOWS you are not happy! Whew. That's not good. Did you give her a chance to say whether she actually did it or not? Did you give her a chance to explain? God wants you to.

Why does God care so much about anger? God's way is for people to listen to others. Give them a chance to explain themselves. Listen quietly, with respect. Control your anger so it doesn't explode in someone else's face. Treat people with love, kindness and respect.

ChallengePoint

OK, it's not easy to control your emotions – especially anger. But God's way is to treat others with love. That means you should swallow your anger and listen to others, keep quiet and do not jump to reactions that make you angry. And ... you can ask God for help.

Know therefore that the LORD your God is God; He is the faithful God, keeping His covenant of love to a thousand generations of those who love Him and keep His commands.

✴ DEUTERONOMY 7:9

Best friends are THE BEST. Seriously, don't you love sleepovers where you stay up late munching on popcorn and sharing your secrets with your friend? Best friends are loyal and promise to keep your secrets. You can trust them, right?

Well, most people are pretty trustworthy and make every effort to keep their promises but sometimes it just doesn't happen. Except for one Person – God. Yep, He is faithful and that means absolutely NOTHING will stop Him from keeping every promise He has made. Get it? NOTHING. Read His Word to learn what those promises are (one of them is to love you totally!).

ChallengePoint

God is faithful. You can always trust Him. Always. He has promised to love you, guide you, protect you, use you in His work, and a zillion other things. Read His Word to discover them. Then, trust Him. If He said it you can bank on it.

Knowing God by
Seeking Salvation

"For God so loved the world that He gave His one and only Son, that whoever believes in Him shall not perish but have eternal life."

✳ JOHN 3:16

A well-written book grabs your attention in the first few pages. You start caring about the main character and what happens to her. If it's a really great book, you can't put it down as you race through it to find out how things turn out. It's a great story!

God has a great story for you, too. His story for you takes you from where you are all the way to heaven – through the salvation He offers you. God sent His only Son, Jesus, to earth. Jesus taught about how to live for God. Then He died for your sins and God raised Him back to life. Accepting Jesus as your Savior is your way to salvation. What a great story!

ChallengePoint

God's salvation story is for you. When you confess your sins and ask Jesus into your heart, then you are saved. Don't just read about it – take action on it.

Knowing God by
Being Thankful

Always use the name of our Lord Jesus Christ to thank God the Father for everything.

✳ EPHESIANS 5:20

When you write thank you cards do you like to decorate them with pictures of hearts and flowers and trees? That's cool. Pretty cards are more fun to read, right? Have you ever thought of writing thank You cards to God? Weird, huh? It could be cool though to make a little book of pictures of all the things you're thankful for.

Why does God want you to be thankful? 'Cause when you start thinking about all the things He does for you, it helps you understand how much He loves you! He just gives and gives and gives to you. Wow. That's worth a picture or two, right?

ChallengePoint

Make a list of your favorite things that God does for you. Maybe you should start a notebook of "I'm thankful for this" pictures to God. Let the thankfulness grow as you understand how much and how often He shows His love to you.

Knowing God by
Celebrating Him

You are worthy, O Lord our God, to receive glory and honor and power. For You created all things, and they exist because You created what You pleased.

✳ REVELATION 4:11

Parties are so much fun! Streamers decorating the room. Balloons, games, cake and ice cream and good friends to celebrate with. Everyone loves a party!

Have you ever had a party to celebrate God? Does that sound odd? Well, why not celebrate God? He created everything there is on this earth and He made it all from nothing! If that doesn't deserve celebrating, what does?

ChallengePoint

OK, you don't have to actually throw a party! But do take time to celebrate God. Need some ideas? Celebrate His incredible creativity. Celebrate His love! Celebrate His guidance in your life! Celebrate the salvation He makes possible! Celebrate Him! As you celebrate all He is and all He does, you will come to understand and appreciate Him more.

Knowing God by
Enduring

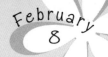

"Lead us not into temptation, but deliver us from the evil one."

✳ MATTHEW 6:13

Temptation is so sneaky … for example, you're just having lunch with a friend when she makes a comment about the new girl in your class … something like "her hair looks like she just came in from a tornado." Or "she must get her clothes at a garbage dump." You say something back that makes your friend laugh and you're both off and running. The temptation to say mean things came camouflaged as a chance to make your friend laugh.

You have to be careful about temptation. Temptation never comes from God. But He will help you fight it off. When you realize you're being tempted, pray this prayer (part of The Lord's Prayer) and ask God to help you be strong. He will always help you. You can endure temptation (that means you can face it but not give in to it) because of His strength in you.

ChallengePoint

Temptation is everywhere – you can count on that. You'll only be able to have victory over it by asking God for help. Ask Him for strength and for help to be kind, loving and obedient. Then, recognize when He helps you in the way you have asked. He will help you endure temptation and stand strong!

Knowing God by
Being Like Christ

"If you want good fruit, you must make the tree good. If your tree is not good, it will have bad fruit. A tree is known by the kind of fruit it produces."

✳ MATTHEW 12:33

Apple picking is fun. You go into an orchard and walk among the apple trees, picking up the scrawny, brown apples from the ground. You especially like the ones that the birds have taken bites from or that have big oozing wormholes in them, right? Yeah, not so much. You want healthy, juicy apples with no worms and no bird bites.

Healthy fruit comes from a healthy tree. The same is true for Christ-followers. See, you can say "Christian" words and even quote Bible verses, but if the way you treat others doesn't match the words, well, that's the bad fruit this verse talks about. How do you learn to be like Christ? Get to know Him – read about His life in the Bible. As you learn about Him you are learning about God and how you should live your life.

ChallengePoint

What's in your heart (good or evil) will come out in the way you live and that is the good and bad fruit that those around you see. Learn to know God by learning to know Christ. That will help make sure your fruit is the good kind.

Knowing God by
Loving Others

"Your love for one another will prove to the world that you are My disciples."

* JOHN 13:35

Members of the same team all dress alike. As you watch a big gymnastics meet, the participating teams march in, all wearing the same warm-up suits. Their team name or the country they represent is plainly displayed on the suit. You can always tell which team an athlete belongs to by what she's wearing.

Did you know there is something that identifies you as a member of God's "team"? Yep, and that thing is love. It is kind of printed on you by the way you treat other people. Your team captain – God – is known for His love for all people. As a member of His team, you should also be loving to others.

ChallengePoint

The hard part of this is that some people are hard to love. In fact, if you had to love them with your own strength it would probably never happen. But with God in your heart, loving those people becomes possible. God is love, let Him love through you!

Knowing God by
Showing Courage

The LORD is my light and my salvation – whom shall I fear? The LORD is the stronghold of my life – of whom shall I be afraid?

✳ PSALM 27:1

During dark stormy nights, when the wind whips tree branches against the windows, you can hear creaks and groans. It's kind of spooky and makes it hard to fall asleep. It helps to have a light on, though. The light makes you feel better because you can see through the shadows and know you are safe.

It's hard to be courageous when you're scared. What does knowing God have to do with fear? With God in your life there is really nothing to be afraid of because He can and will protect you from whatever dangers come into your life. God is more powerful than anything else in the world and He loves you more than anything else. So, what is there to be afraid of?

ChallengePoint

It's OK to be afraid – nothing wrong with that. But remember that God is taking care of you. Think about God's power – it created everything there is. His power controls nature, ocean waves, lightning and wind. Think about His power that raised Christ back to life from being dead. All of that power is on your side. His power will protect you if you just ask Him.

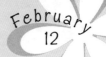
Each of you has received a gift to use to serve others. Be good servants of God's various gifts of grace.

* 1 PETER 4:10

Presents are the best! Do you like great big packages with big fancy bows or do you like the mystery of small presents? Sometimes the best things come in small packages. How would you feel about opening a package and finding a gift that can only be used for others? Not a normal kind of gift, huh? But God gives you gifts like that. There are things you can do or be (like a loyal friend) that are the way God wants you to serve Him.

God has this gigantic supply of abilities that He passes out to each person. The reason? It's incredible, but God wants our help to get His work done here on earth. Yep, He lets us plain old human beings help Him with His plans for what He wants to happen on earth.

ChallengePoint

Do you find it amazing that God gives you gifts that are for His work? Well, He does and He wants you to share those gifts with people around you. Are you willing to give God your time and energy?

Knowing God by
Trusting Him

The LORD is my strength and my shield; my heart trusts in Him, and I am helped. My heart leaps for joy and I will give thanks to Him in song.

✳ PSALM 28:7

OK, honesty time. Think about a hard time in your life: Some older girl picking on you on the school bus, family problems, illness, death of a loved one, moving to a new school … or about a thousand other things. What's your first reaction in a hard situation? Panic? Fear? How often do you burst out in song? Yeah, not so often when you're scared or hurting, right?

You see, the thing about trust is that trust is only trust in the hard times of life. Get it? Anyone can claim to trust God when things are going great – seriously, why do you even need trust when everything is great? But when life is really stinky and you can believe God will get you through and protect you and guide you – that's trust.

ChallengePoint

Trust is what you should work toward. If you don't go right to trust every time you have a problem, that's OK. Hopefully you get there eventually and the more you experience that you can trust God, the more you will be able to trust Him the next time.

I am convinced that nothing can ever separate us from God's love. No power in the sky above or in the earth below – indeed, nothing in all creation will ever be able to separate us from the love of God that is revealed in Christ Jesus our Lord.

✳ ROMANS 8:38-39

E-mail, IM, cell phones, text messaging … staying in touch with loved ones is easier now than ever before. Just imagine if your best friend moved 1,000 miles away and the only way you could hear from her was through hand-written letters that took weeks to get to her. But you can e-mail, IM, call or text and have an instant conversation. You may be separated by distance, but you're together in conversation.

Did you know that nothing can separate you from God's love? In fact, He is even closer than IM – He's in your heart. You can talk to Him any time! Even more important, NOTHING and no one can ever pull you away from His love.

ChallengePoint

Yes, it's true that nothing can separate you from God's love. The only thing … the ONLY thing that can get in the way of God's love for you is … you. Yep, His love is constant and steady and there for you to receive and enjoy. So … do you?

"Ask and it will be given to you; seek and you will find; knock and the door will be opened to you."

* MATTHEW 7:7

Honesty time – how long does your Christmas list get? Do you get everything on your list? Probably not. Your parents know that it's not good to give you everything you ask for. How about God? Does He give you everything you ask for? Does this verse mean that all you have to do is ask and BAM, God does it? Nope. So what does it mean? Asking God for help shows your dependence on Him. God wants you to depend on Him. He wants you to tell Him the desires of your heart.

When you talk to God and read His Word every day your desires start to change. As you get to know Him better and spend more time with Him, your heart tends to become more like His. This verse is written to people who know God. Those who want to grow hearts like His.

ChallengePoint

This verse assumes a journey like this: Know God. Once you know God, tell Him the desires of your heart (things that your heart really wants) – and keep on telling Him. Read His Word, think about Him and notice how He grows your heart to be like His. Pretty soon you'll want what He wants.

Seeking His Protection

We know that in everything God works for the good of those who love Him. They are the people He called, because that was His plan.

* ROMANS 8:28

You and your best friend have been best friends for, like, forever. You tell each other everything, laugh at the same things, like the same food, music, books. You are pretty much always together ... until she seems to find a new friend and all of a sudden you feel pretty alone and very much on the outside. It hurts. In fact, it stinks. Where is God when life stinks? The answer is that He's right where He's always been – with you.

God doesn't cause bad things to happen, but He doesn't ignore them either. He will help you through them. He can even turn them into something good. God loves you and wants to teach you to be a better person and a stronger Christ-follower. So, no experience – good or bad – is wasted. God will teach you through all of it.

ChallengePoint

When life gets tough, what should you do? The temptation is to get depressed or angry. Instead, try looking for where you can see God in the situation. Remember, He loves you a lot and you're not alone. He'll help you.

Knowing God by
Serving Him

Feed the hungry, and help those in trouble. Then your light will shine out from the darkness, and the darkness around you will be as bright as noon.

※ ISAIAH 58:10

Every town has people who are hungry. You may not know it, but it might be a neighbor or someone in your school. There are people everywhere who need help. Big things like tsunamis, earthquakes, hurricanes or tornadoes that rip up homes and kill people are big news. Christians around the world pray for those who lost their homes, family members and virtually everything they own.

Praying is good and certainly an important part of caring for others. But God expects more. When someone is hungry or homeless or ill or has some other problem, they need real help. And it's not just people who suffer the big calamities; people every day are hungry and homeless. They need your help.

ChallengePoint

As a kid there are some things you can't do. But as God's child you can work with others and even motivate others to help people in need in practical ways. There may be homeless shelters or food pantries right in your town that always need help. See how you can put your faith into action!

Knowing God by
Obeying Him

"Don't worship any other god, because I, the LORD, the Jealous One, am a jealous God."

✳ EXODUS 34:14

Do you have a favorite singer? Is there one that you and your friends go gaa-gaa over? Do you have posters with his or her picture plastered all over your room? It's OK to be a fan of a musician. As long as you keep that in perspective and don't make your fandom more important than God.

What does obeying have to do with God being jealous? It has to do with who your heart belongs to. As this verse says, God insists on being Number One in your heart – the most important, the One you honor, respect, follow and obey. If He isn't Number One, then you might say, "Yeah, I love God," but then think about things that don't honor Him or be selfish or mean to others. In other words, you will not really serve and love Him. God won't stand for that. He wants all your heart and all your worship.

ChallengePoint

Is God Number One in your life? More important than anyone else? Even your big music dude? If He's not, you're wasting your time. God is a jealous God and will not take second place to anyone else.

Knowing God by
Confessing Sin

But if we confess our sins, He will forgive our sins, because we can trust God to do what is right. He will cleanse us from all the wrongs we have done.

✻ 1 JOHN 1:9

If I tell you something, will you promise to still be my friend? Promise?" Is that how you confess things to your friends? How about to your parents? "If I tell you this, will you still love me?" OK, maybe you wouldn't say that out loud, but do those thoughts run through your mind?

Aren't you glad you don't EVER have to think that where God is concerned? The thing is, God wants to forgive you for your sins. So, when you confess them, He is like, "Yahoo. Now I can forgive you!" OK, maybe God doesn't really say "Yahoo." But He does forgive. He wants to!

ChallengePoint

Confession gets things out in the open. It clears the air. You come to God; He forgives. All is well. Your relationship with Him, which was blocked because of your sin, is wide open again. God loves you. He wants to forgive your sins and wipe the slate clean. That starts with your confession.

His Forgiveness

Be kind and loving to each other, and forgive each other just as God forgave you in Christ.

∗ EPHESIANS 4:32

God is pretty clear on His feelings about forgiveness … just do it. When you think about it, God forgives you … every day. So, if you turn around and refuse to forgive someone who hurt you, then why should you expect God (or anyone else) to forgive you?

Or (and this is much more girl-like, isn't it?) what if you "forgive" but keep that hurt tucked away in your heart to throw back in the person's face somewhere down the road when she hurts you again. She asks forgiveness again but you come out with, "Oh yeah, you say you're sorry, but six years ago you did this or that!" Not good. God willingly forgives you … again and again. Pass that along to others. It's the God way of living.

ChallengePoint

How good are you at forgiving others? It takes a non-self-centered viewpoint to accept someone's apology and then completely forgive and forget. Make it your goal to focus on loving others the way God loves you. Forgiveness comes more easily when you do that.

Knowing God by
Seeking His Guidance

Trust in the LORD with all your heart; do not depend on your own understanding. Seek His will in all you do, and He will show you which path to take.

✳ PROVERBS 3:5-6

From whom do you take your cues as to what's cool … what's "in?" Some girls pay a lot of attention to older girls they admire. Some read magazines or check certain websites to see what the hot topics and styles are.

You need to be so careful about where you take your guidance from because other people, who don't care a bit about God, can really take you down the wrong path. The cool thing about God is that He never leaves you on your own. He loves you so He keeps an eye on you all the time. When you ask Him for guidance, He will help you.

ChallengePoint

God's guidance is a whole lot better than trying to figure things out for yourself because God sees a bigger picture than you do. You might be trying to solve just the problem of the moment, but He knows what you're going to need tomorrow, next week and next year. The hard part is waiting for His guidance when you have asked for help. Be patient, wait for Him to tell you what to do. He's a lot smarter than you are!

A fool shows his annoyance at once, but a prudent man overlooks an insult.

✳ PROVERBS 12:16

Some people have a short fuse – anger explodes out of them like fireworks blasting into the sky. People around them are caught off guard and usually hurt by the explosion.

A quick temper explodes when you're not expecting it. Maybe you think it should be OK to blow up at someone who insults you. Sorry, but God says that's not the way it should be. A fool explodes – a wise person stays calm.

Why? 'Cause that shows that you want to please and honor God. That's wise.

ChallengePoint

Are you an exploder or a calm person? If you have a tendency to explode then maybe you need to ask God to help you be more calm and less reactive to situations. Be wise – stay calm.

Knowing God by
His Faithfulness

"I have told you this, so that you might have peace in your hearts because of Me. While you are in the world, you will have to suffer. But cheer up! I have defeated the world."

✳ JOHN 16:33

Have you ever done a zip line? You start high up on a platform, then slide down a cable to the ground. Sound scary? Well, it could be except you're hooked into that harness. It will catch you if you start to fall from the line. God's faithfulness is kind of like that harness. It protects you from falling away from God when life gets tough.

Life can get pretty tough sometimes – family troubles, parents divorcing, illness of a loved one, friends moving away – but God is faithful. That means He is right there with you through your problems. He may not stop them from happening, but He will walk through them with you. He's more powerful than any problem.

ChallengePoint

It's easy for someone to say "just trust God." But it isn't easy to trust that something good will come out of a really painful problem. Having a history with God where you can look back and see how He has been faithful helps you trust Him more with current problems. So, if you're facing some big problem right now; look back and see how God helped you in the past.

The payment for sin is death. But God gives us the free gift of life forever in Christ Jesus our Lord.

* ROMANS 6:23

Certain things are just givens – dogs bark; cats meow, chickens cluck, people sin. Yep, everyone since Adam and Eve sins. You can deny it or try to justify your actions, but the plain old truth is that you sin. That means you do things that break God's laws.

Sin is serious and there is punishment for it – death. God doesn't fool around when it comes to sin. You sin, you die forever – no heaven. WAIT, that's not completely true because God loves you. So, He offers the gift of life forever with Him. The gift is free to you. It cost Him something – the pain and the very life of His only Son – but He did it anyway. Why? Read it again … HE LOVES YOU!

ChallengePoint

Salvation is possible only because God loves you. It's available because Jesus was willing to pay the price for your sins. It's free because that's how much God loves you. He wants you to be with Him forever in heaven … alive. That's salvation and it saves you from the death caused by your sins.

Knowing God by
Being Thankful

It is good to give thanks to the LORD, to sing praises to the Most High. It is good to proclaim Your unfailing love in the morning, Your faithfulness in the evening.

✳ PSALM 92:1-2

Fan letters are written to movie stars, musicians and artists – pretty much anyone who does things for the public receives fan mail. These letters sing the praises of the skills that have been shared and thank the artist for his or her influence in the letter writer's life.

Fan letters are pretty cool. Why don't you write one to God? Tell Him how awesome His work is and thank Him for all He does! By doing this you will take time to think about all the ways He shows His love for you and the words of thanks will fill your fan letter!

ChallengePoint

Just as this verse suggests, it's a good idea to start your day with thanking God for His love. Thank Him for some specific way He shows His love to you. End your day with thanks to Him too. See how your relationship with Him grows and changes as you live in thankfulness.

Clap your hands, all you people. Shout to God with joy.

✳ PSALM 47:1

Have you ever done a happy dance? You see different forms of the happy dance at concerts, football games and pretty much anywhere people gather. Lift your arms in the air and celebrate God. Celebrate all He is, does, and how He loves you!

Here's some ideas to get you started:

He created everything … EVERYTHING. That means:

- The earth
- The sun
- The moon and stars
- Water
- The oceans
- The mountains
- Grass
- Every animal you can think of
- Air
- Trees and flowers
- People … that means YOU
- Your family and friends
- He sent Jesus which means you can have salvation
- The Bible and Prayer

Well, that should get you started. Celebrate God and all He gives!

ChallengePoint

Let your heart fill with joy toward God. Enjoy it and celebrate the many ways He shows His love to you!

Knowing God by
Enduring

We can rejoice, too, when we run into problems and trials, for we know that they help us develop endurance. And endurance develops strength of character, and character strengthens our confident hope of salvation. We know how dearly God loves us, because He has given us the Holy Spirit to fill our hearts with His love.

✳ ROMANS 5:3-5

Being punished stinks. It's no fun. But you know that if you disobey your parents, punishment will come – being grounded, privileges taken away, extra chores … Why? Because that's how you'll learn from your mistake. It may surprise you to know that it makes them sad to punish you, but in the long run it's the right thing to do.

That is also true in your relationship with God. He loves you, and He wants you to grow into a mature, wise young woman. However, the only way to become mature is through tough times. So, when things get hard, remember that God may be trying to teach you something.

ChallengePoint

No one likes punishment and it's not easy to be happy about problems. But try to understand how God is growing you into a stronger and more responsible person who will become a stronger and more mature Christian.

Being Like Christ

Set your minds on things above, not on earthly things.

* COLOSSIANS 3:2

When you settle down with your friends at lunch time, what do you talk about? What's your favorite thing to think about when you're just relaxing – what's the movie in your mind that *you* are starring in? Whatever fills your thoughts most of the time is going to show in the way you live and in what you consider to be important.

What did Christ think about when He was on earth? How to help others know God better. How to show kindness and love to them. He pretty much focused all of His thoughts in those areas. He did not think about Himself or His comforts. So, if being like Christ and showing love to others, being helpful and kind is on your mind, well, that's the kind of stuff you'll do. So, think on the things of heaven – the things that will make you more like Christ.

ChallengePoint

This may come pretty easily to you because you are basically a kind and loving girl. That's great! Remember that as you are doing these things you are showing the love of Christ to those around you!

All things grow with love.

~ ANONYMOUS

March

Knowing God by
Loving Others

No one has ever seen God. But if we love each other, God lives in us, and His love is brought to full expression in us.

* 1 JOHN 4:12

Do you enjoy looking at photos of your parents as children? In many families you can put childhood pictures of mom and dad next to pictures of their children and see a big resemblance. Sometimes it's even hard to tell which picture is mom or dad and which one is the child. Family resemblance is a cool thing! Even cooler is your resemblance to your Father God.

But since He is a Spirit, how do you know if you look like Him? Actually, there's an easy answer to that. People who show love to others, are kind and considerate and think of others first, look like God. You see, God loves people. Of course, He wants people to obey Him and love Him back, but He keeps on loving them even if they don't. So, you show what God is like by loving others.

ChallengePoint

How are you at unselfish and considerate love? Of course, it's easy with your friends, but what about loving people who don't treat you well? Yeah, that's when it gets hard to love like God does. But that's when it counts.

Because He Himself suffered when He was tempted, He is able to help those who are being tempted.

* HEBREWS 2:18

You and a friend settle down in your room with a big bowl of popcorn and a couple of soft drinks and you talk for hours and hours. Why can you talk so long? Because you have a lot in common. Maybe you both struggle with the same math issues. Both of you might know someone who is seriously ill. Whatever it is, you can talk forever because you understand each other.

Have you ever wanted to say to God, "You don't know what life is like down here!" Sometimes temptations are so strong and intense that they are hard to fight. Jesus faced every kind of temptation you will ever have to face and He never gave in. Yes, He is God, that's why it's so cool that He wants to help you fight temptation. You can use His strength to fight it.

ChallengePoint

Temptations happen. There's no way around it. But if you turn to God for help you can fight it off. He loves you and promises to be there for you.

Knowing God by
Witnessing His Power

There are things about Him that people cannot see – His eternal power and all the things that make Him God. But since the beginning of the world those things have been easy to understand by what God has made. So people have no excuse for the bad things they do.

* ROMANS 1:20

For some reason, Missouri is known as the Show Me state. Supposedly people who live in Missouri have to see proof before they will believe things. Well, when it comes to seeing God's power, that's an easy thing!

There's plenty of evidence of His power in the world. Look at the sun, moon and zillions of stars in the sky. Look at the mountains and oceans, powerful waterfalls, powerful weather, tiny flowers that push up through soil. God's creation shows His power and leaves no doubt that He is eternal.

ChallengePoint

Understanding God's power is important because it gives you something to hold on to when the world goes crazy. The news is filled with reports of wars and murders. There are terrible natural disasters. The world can be a scary place so you need to know that God's power is greater than anything else. His power is there for you. He loves you.

Faith means being sure of the things we hope for and knowing that something is real even if we do not see it.

* HEBREWS 11:1

There are various computer programs that let a person do amazing things with photographs. Pieces of photographs can be cut and pasted together so seamlessly that the end result looks like an original photo. It's hard to know what to believe.

God doesn't need anything like that. He is honest and powerful. What the Bible tells you about God and His work is absolutely true. He doesn't do any cutting and pasting with His promises.

When you know Him and trust Him you can have faith in everything the Bible tells you about Him – even though you can't see God you can have faith in Him.

ChallengePoint

It's impossible to know God without faith. Faith is believing and trusting, even in what you can't see. You can have faith in God and in what the Bible tells you about Him. What God says about Himself in the Bible is the absolute truth. He never lies or pads the truth. You can believe.

Knowing God by
Giving

"I tell you the truth," Jesus said, "this poor widow has given more than all the rest of them. For they have given a tiny part of their surplus, but she, poor as she is, has given everything she has."

✳ LUKE 21:3-4

You probably know of missionaries your church supports. Some of them live in distant lands. Foreign missionaries move away from their homes and give their lives completely to God's work. Giving to God comes in different forms. In this verse, Jesus is commenting on a woman who gave all the money she had to God's work. She didn't just give a little or even split it 50-50 with Him. She gave it all.

That kind of devotion is exactly what God wants from you. OK, maybe you don't have a lot of money to give. This verse doesn't even mean that you give every cent to God. It means that you give your whole heart to Him. When you do that your money will be used in the way God wants.

ChallengePoint

Don't hold back from God. That means don't think you can be devoted to God on Sunday but on Tuesday you can do whatever you want. Give your whole heart to God every day. Be willing to give whatever God asks for!

Suppressing Our Pride

"Be careful! When you do good things, don't do them in front of people to be seen by them. If you do that, you will have no reward from your Father in heaven."

✳ MATTHEW 6:1

It's called "tooting your own horn" when a person feels the need to let everyone know how wonderful she is. A girl like this wants to be the leader in her group. She wants others to follow her, copy her, do what she says and like whom she likes. She wants to be in charge and she doesn't really care who she hurts or pushes around.

That's not God's way. God often makes a point in His Word of how important it is to Him that people love one another. He wants you to do nice things for others because you love Him. That requires a pureness in your heart that God will see as your motivation. Now, God is serious about this. So girls who push others around will only get praise from others – not from God.

ChallengePoint

God wants your motivation to be right – obeying Him, loving Him and loving others. If your motivation for what you do comes from anywhere else … you're toast. Don't count on any reward from Him. If power over others is what you're all about – then that's all the reward you're going to get.

Knowing God by
Trusting in Him

Trusting unfaithful people when you are in trouble is like eating with a broken tooth or walking with a crippled foot.

* PROVERBS 25:19

Have you watched the girls on your country's national gymnastics team compete? Those girls can fling their bodies around in amazing contortions at impressive heights. When a gymnast is first learning those skills they are taking some risks. If you're flying through the air upside down you want to be sure you land right. The gymnast has to completely trust that her coach will catch her if she falls. She would never trust a younger, weaker girl to be ready to catch her. Trusting someone who isn't dependable would not be smart.

People are never as dependable as God is and un-qualified people are definitely not dependable! Just as a gymnast trusts only her coach, you should trust only God for direction and guidance in your life.

ChallengePoint

It's OK to have friends who give you advice. It's even good to talk things through with others when you have trouble. But never, never, never trust anyone more than you trust God. He's the wisest One and He loves you very much. You can depend on God … always.

God can bless you with everything you need, and you will always have more than enough to do all kinds of good things for others. The Scriptures say, "God freely gives His gifts to the poor, and always does right."

✳ 2 CORINTHIANS 9:8-9

Who doesn't love Christmas? In some families the gifts are passed out so each person has a big stack of presents in front of them before the packages are ripped open. It's pretty cool to get gifts. Who gives you the best gifts? Well, God gives you a lot. In fact, everything you have ultimately comes from God. He made everything there is.

Maybe you've been super-blessed and have a very comfortable life. What does God want you to do with what you have? Share it. Yep, He gives you what you need and wants you to share with others so they have what they need too. It's kind of a "pay it forward" sort of thing.

ChallengePoint

The reality is that no person is alone in this world and no one should feel as though they are. God instructs His children to help one another and look out for one another. So, whatever you have – however much you have – find someone to share it with.

Knowing God by
His Love

"Teach these new disciples to obey all the commands I have given you. And be sure of this: I am with you always, even to the end of the age."

* MATTHEW 28:20

It would be awesome if people you love could promise that they will never, ever leave you. They can't. All humans will die eventually. Not much we can do about that. Beyond that, sometimes friends stop being friends. Sometimes families break up and one parent leaves (even though their love for you doesn't stop). Sometimes when the going gets tough … people leave.

One of the ways you can know God loves you totally is that He will never, ever leave you. Never. He promises. God's love is incredibly strong and He will stick with you no matter how tough life gets; regardless of whether you love Him back or not. He wants you to obey Him and do His work, of course. But even if times happen when you don't … He doesn't leave you. He never will.

ChallengePoint

When you think about it, God's promise to be with you always is a great motivation to return His love, isn't it? Seriously, if He loves you that much and promises to always stick with you … how can you help but love Him back?

"If My people, who are called by My name, will humble themselves and pray and seek My face and turn from their wicked ways, then will I hear from heaven and will forgive their sin and will heal their land."

✲ 2 CHRONICLES 7:14

Prayer is … talking. There are several different ways of talking – face to face conversation, e-mail, IM, texting and … prayer. Whatever your chosen way of talking, you probably do it a lot. Prayer, though, is talking with God.

What an honor it is that God promises to hear your prayers and answer them according to His will. But look at the characteristics of the praying person given in this verse: humbleness (that means not demanding your way), seeking God's face (that means listening for what He wants), turning from wicked ways (Wow, that means a lot of things, such as not being selfish and trusting God).

ChallengePoint

Are the three characteristics given in this verse true of you? Do you approach God in those ways or are you sometimes a demanding, bossy girl? God wants to hear your prayers, wants to forgive your sins, wants to do amazing things for you. Do your part and approach Him with the respect and love He deserves.

Knowing God by
Seeking His Protection

"God blesses those people who grieve. They will find comfort!"
   * MATTHEW 5:4

Loss … hurts. You know that if a person you loved has died. You know that if a dearly loved pet has run away. You know that if you've lost some item that you loved a lot. When you lose someone or something special, you grieve for it. Have you ever thought that you need protection when you're mourning? Weird, huh? Generally you think of protection as being kept safe from danger or safe in a storm – not when your heart is hurting. It's true though. When you are grieving your resistance is down. That's a perfect time for Satan to creep into your heart and set up residence, keeping you away from God.

When you're hurting, turn to God for comfort and He will protect your tender heart. He will comfort you and keep Satan far away while your grief heals.

ChallengePoint

It would be nice if God just did away with all hurt, right? He doesn't do that but you can always remember this: (1) God loves you. (2) He's always there for you. That doesn't mean that life will always be easy or that you will never hurt. It just means that He will protect you through whatever pain life brings.

Knowing God by
Serving Him

"Good people bring good things out of their hearts, but evil people bring evil things out of their hearts."

* MATTHEW 12:35

Mm, one of the best things in the world is warm-from-the-oven chocolate chip cookies. But what if when that cookie batter was mixed up, instead of sugar the baker put black pepper in the dough? Wow, that would change the flavor a lot and the warm-from-the-oven cookies would not be so great. What you put in the dough determines the flavor of the cookie.

Serving God has the same formula. The kinds of things you put into your heart determines what kind of service comes out of it. From a healthy heart that honors and serves God comes loving service to God and others. God wants your service, and He will help keep your heart obedient and healthy. He will help you learn to love Him and others more.

ChallengePoint

What's truly in your heart will come out in the way you live. If your heart is healthy and filled with love and kindness that's what will come out. If you're a self-centered girl whose heart focuses on yourself, that will show in how you treat others and God. This verse reminds you to serve God from a healthy heart.

Knowing God by
Obeying Him

The fear of the LORD is the beginning of wisdom; all who follow His precepts have good understanding. To Him belongs eternal praise.

* PSALM 111:10

R-E-S-P-E-C-T. That's what it's all about. You see, fear in this verse doesn't actually mean shaking-in-your-boots-scared-silly of God. It means respecting and honoring Him in a way He deserves because, He is, after all, God. That kind of fear is the beginning of being smart.

True respect for God is where obedience begins. To obey God's commandments you have to know them and that means reading His Word – the Bible. A truly smart person knows God's commandments and obeys them. By doing that you get smarter and smarter!

ChallengePoint

If you're going to be obedient, you have to know what is right and wrong. Reading God's Word is the best place to learn that. Study God's Word and obey the commandments you find there. Then you will be wise and will grow more and more wise with each day.

Knowing God by
Obeying Him

*If you obey every law except one, you are still guilty of breaking
them all.*

> * JAMES 2:10

Do you compare yourself to other people? Do you look
at how one girl treats her parents and think, "OK, I'm a
little more respectful than she is?" Do you notice someone
cheating on a test and think, "I'm better than her, 'cause I
never cheat?"

When it comes to the whole obeying God thing, you
may feel like you're doing pretty well. You can usually
find someone who is a lot worse than you. Well, here's
the thing – even if you only break ONE of God's laws,
in God's eyes, you might as well have broken all of
them. Why does the Bible say that? Because God wants
complete obedience from His children. He doesn't put
up with disobedience. He doesn't play the comparison
game and He doesn't grade on the curve. You stand alone
based on your own obedience.

ChallengePoint

Is this news to you? Did you think you were doing OK by just
obeying the easy stuff? It's good to obey as much as you can,
but do not ever be satisfied with just being pretty good. Keep
learning and growing and obeying more and more.

Knowing God by
His Forgiveness

"Even if that person wrongs you seven times a day and each time turns again and asks forgiveness, you must forgive."

✻ LUKE 17:4

Drama. Life with your friends is probably filled with the drama of "She said this," or "She said that," and then everyone gets mad and stops talking to one friend for a while. When someone hurts you, how many times does God expect you to forgive her? Well, this Scripture verse says … a lot! Why would God ask you to be so forgiving and patient? Simple – because He is.

Stop and think about how many times God forgives you. Seriously, how many times a day do you have unkind thoughts? What about feelings of pride? How often do you talk back to your mom or complain about rules? Now, how often does God forgive you for those things? Do you know the answer to that? Every single time.

ChallengePoint

God is forgiving because He loves you. When you ask for His forgiveness, He will give it every time – even seven times a day. He asks you to pass that same forgiving spirit along to others and forgive them. It's God's way.

I will instruct you and teach you in the way you should go; I will counsel you and watch over you.

* PSALM 32:8

If you've ever traveled to a foreign country you know the confusion of not being able to speak the language of the people. Road signs are in a language you can't read. You can't ask directions because you can't understand the answer. You need a guide; someone who speaks and reads the language of the country.

You need a life-guide, too, someone who understands the big picture of living in this world, following God's commands, and loving others. Who could do that for you? God. He promised to guide you. He knows what's best for you because He can see the big picture of your life from when you were in diapers all the way to the end of your life. So ask Him for guidance. He will give it.

ChallengePoint

Why put yourself through the agony of trying to figure out things you don't understand? God already has a plan for your life. You know it's a good plan because He loves you so much. Just ask Him to guide you and then follow His plan.

Knowing God by
His Faithfulness

I am certain that God, who began the good work within you, will continue His work until it is finally finished on the day when Christ Jesus returns.

✳ PHILIPPIANS 1:6

Look through your baby pictures. Were you a cutie? Look at how tiny you were. Maybe you weighed 7 or 8 pounds and were 20 or 21 inches long when you were born. Look at pictures of you through the years and how you've grown. Isn't it amazing that everything your body needs to be a full-grown adult was there on the day you were born? God has continued the work of growing your body and maturing it as the years pass.

Just as wonderful as your body growing, from the minute you asked Jesus into your heart God started working in it. He started teaching you and guiding you in how to live for Him and be a good example to those around you.

ChallengePoint

If God can plan for your body to have everything it needs to grow from a baby to an adult, He can also plan for your spirit to grow and mature in your faith. God loves you very much, so He sticks close to you – forever. He teaches you and trains you and more than anything else loves you throughout your life!

Knowing God by
Enduring

Your words came to me, and I listened carefully to them. Your words made me very happy, because I am called by Your name, LORD God All-Powerful.

✳ JEREMIAH 15:16

Good nutrition is taught in school and probably at home too. Healthy food gives your body the fuel it needs to grow up strong and healthy. Junk food doesn't give your body that fuel. Good food has a long-term effect. If you eat junk food all the time, you might feel OK now, but if you think about the future – like 20 years from now – you may pay the price for today's poor nutrition.

Your heart and soul have the same issue. To be able to stand strong for God, you've got to feed your soul healthy food now. That "good food" comes from God's Word. Read the Bible. Read it over and over. Memorize it so it's tucked away in your heart. You'll never be sorry.

ChallengePoint

There are constant temptations to turn away from God. They are subtle things that don't seem to matter a lot ... except they do because they open the door to more things that are disobedient to God's will. The only way to endure with God – to stay strong – is to read and learn God's Word.

Knowing God by
Being Like Christ

The LORD hates every liar, but He is the friend of all who can be trusted.

* PROVERBS 12:22

What if your good friend's new haircut looks awful? Should you just be nice and say, "Oh wow, it's awesome!" This is tough, but what would Jesus do? He'd be nice, but honest. Like, you could say, "Wonder how it would look if it was a little shorter?" That doesn't endorse the new cut, but doesn't criticize it either.

Being like Christ is a big order, isn't it? After all, Christ was perfect, so how could you possibly be like Him? You can take it in steps. For example, as this verse tells you … don't lie. Christ was always truthful – kind, but truthful. Read through the Gospels – you won't find Him saying what He thinks people want to hear. He was honest. So, take one small step by being truthful. Honesty pleases God and it's the fairest thing for other people too.

ChallengePoint

It's hard to be truthful sometimes because you want people to like you, right? Stop it. Be courageous – be honest. It's the Jesus way.

Knowing God by
Being Like Christ

Not that I was ever in need, for I have learned how to be content with whatever I have.

✳ PHILIPPIANS 4:11

Contentment is not promoted in the media today. From clothes, perfumes, technology and hair stuff, even to books about God and new Bible versions – advertising tells you there's lots of stuff that you "need."

Everyone fights "give it to me" thoughts at some point in their lives because we live in a world that puts a lot of importance on stuff. Many people feel that the people with the most stuff are the winners in life. God doesn't agree. Becoming more like Christ means finding that place of peace in your life where you're happy where you are and with what you've got. One of the reasons you can find that peaceful place – the main reason – is because you know you have God and He is enough.

ChallengePoint

Everything you hear on television and read in magazines and on the Internet, and maybe even what you hear from your friends, is bombarding you with the pressure to GET MORE STUFF. Having more stuff is a status symbol in this world. But it isn't a sign of success with God. In fact, success as far as God is concerned is contentment and peace with what you have.

Knowing God by
Loving Your Friends

Two people are better than one, because they get more done by working together. If one falls down, the other can help him up. But it is bad for the person who is alone and falls, because no one is there to help.

* ECCLESIASTES 4:9-10

Best friends are … the best! Your best friend probably likes the same things you like and you have a lot in common so you can talk for hours about stuff. When you and your best friend are "clicking" (agreeing and getting along) you feel like you're connected and can take on the world!

What a great idea God had to give you friends! Did you ever think about that? Your best friend is a gift from God. What's more, that friend is evidence of God's love for you. God knew you wouldn't want to be alone. He knew life would be more fun with friends. He knew you could be stronger with a friend by your side to help you and to love you in the hard times of life.

ChallengePoint

Thank God right now for your friends … especially your best friend. She is God's gift to you. Because God loves you He gave you people in your life to help you and to have fun with you. He knew that would mean a lot to you.

Loving Others

We love because He first loved us.

✳ 1 JOHN 4:19

Learning new information often involves reading. Books on world history give you a lot of information as to how countries have developed to where they are today. There's an old saying that Christians (that's you) may be the only "Bible" some people read.

In other words, people who would never read the Bible learn what God is like by how you live. Hopefully they will see love in you. Not just love for people who are like you, but love for all people.

One person's acts of love cause a chain reaction of kindness. That's how God's love affects people. When one person actually understands how much God loves her then she shows love to others. It's like setting up rows of dominoes and then knocking over the first one, which hits the next, which hits the next … until they all fall. God's love is contagious. When you get a glimpse of how much He loves you, you can't help but pass it on.

ChallengePoint

Remember you are a walking, talking Bible and may be the only way that some people ever get a glimpse of God's love. Some people will see God's love – through you.

Knowing God by
Showing Courage

"I give you peace, the kind of peace that only I can give. It isn't like the peace that this world can give. So don't be worried or afraid."

* JOHN 14:27

Umbrellas are a great invention, aren't they? It's so peaceful to take a walk in a nice gentle rain with a big umbrella over you, protecting you from the rain. It keeps away all the wet stuff. Pretty cool.

The peace God gives is a kind of umbrella. It hovers over you and around you, protecting you from fear and worry – if you let it. The ability to actually be courageous comes only when you have peace about who is in control of your life.

When you know that God is running things, you can have peace of mind and heart, regardless of what's going on around you.

ChallengePoint

People who don't know God won't understand this kind of peace. But it's the best kind. You don't have to worry. You don't have to be afraid. Just pop open that umbrella of peace that comes from letting God watch over you and you can be at peace.

"You will receive power when the Holy Spirit comes upon you. You will be My witnesses, telling people about Me everywhere – in Jerusalem, throughout Judea, in Samaria, and to the ends of the earth."

* Acts 1:8

You may not know much about how cars work. But you probably have heard lots of grown-ups talking about the price of gasoline these days. The thing is that most cars have to have gas to run. Burning the gas is what gives them the power to go. Without gas most cars just become really big lawn decorations.

You need power to run too – God's power. His power comes to you through the presence of the Holy Spirit in you. Is that kind of a hard concept to understand? That's because the Holy Spirit is a … Spirit. God's Spirit comes to live in your heart and gives you power to do the work God has chosen for you to do. Pretty cool, huh? You don't have to worry about becoming a really big lawn decoration because the Holy Spirit lives in you.

ChallengePoint

If you've asked Jesus into your heart, God's Spirit is living in you right now. That means His power is there for you. When you need help, just ask God for it. His Spirit will guide you.

Knowing God by
His Love

"The greatest love a person can show is to die for his friends."

✳ JOHN 15:13

You would probably do just about anything for your family or your really close friends. If any of them are in trouble, you would help in any way possible. If they need help, you would give it. That's what love does, right? It gives and gives to help those you love.

God's love for you is the best example of this giving love. He held nothing back in His effort to show His love. His love for you is so great that He sent His only Son, Jesus, to earth. Jesus lived on the earth for 33 years, teaching about how to live for God and love Him; teaching about how to show love to other people.

Jesus held nothing back, in fact, He died for you. That's total and complete love.

ChallengePoint

God's love for you is complete. He holds nothing back. How does your love for Him measure up? Do you hold some parts of your life back from Him or have you given Him your whole heart?

Devote yourselves to prayer, being watchful and thankful.

* COLOSSIANS 4:2

Do you pray with your eyes open? That's kind of a strange question, isn't it? But look at this verse – it instructs you to pray (a lot) and watch at the same time. What does that mean? It doesn't necessarily mean keeping your eyes open. It does mean to pay attention. Don't just bombard God with your requests, pay attention to what He is doing and how He is answering your prayers.

Being watchful with thanksgiving will help you to notice what He's doing and give Him thanks.

ChallengePoint

Don't make your prayer life a long list of "do this and do that" for God. And don't pray in a half-hearted way. Devote yourselves to prayer. Believe that God will answer. Constant prayer will help you get to know God better and you will be able to see Him working in your life.

Knowing God by
Seeking His Protection

Jesus said, "Come to Me, all of you who are weary and carry heavy burdens, and I will give you rest."

* MATTHEW 11:28

What kinds of things get you down? Maybe it's some of these:

- Friends who are loyal one day and stab you in the back the next.
- Trouble concentrating on school things resulting in bad grades.
- Pressure to try drugs or alcohol.
- Parents who fight all the time.

This list would be longer if you added your own struggles to it. So … what do you do? How do you deal with these things? Jesus has the answer. He cares about your problems. He knows life gets pretty tough sometimes and He promises to help.

ChallengePoint

Jesus promises rest from the problems and stresses of life. If you come to Him and ask Him for help, He will give it. You just have to trust Him to give it, and wait for it.

Knowing God by
Serving Him

Jesus said, "Come follow Me, and I will make you fish for people."
So Simon and Andrew immediately left their nets and followed
him.

✳ MATTHEW 4:19-20

There is a progression of important things that happened in these two Scripture verses: 1. Jesus spoke. 2. People listened. 3. Jesus gave instructions. 4. People obeyed.

Jesus said this to men who earned their livings by fishing. He asked them to leave their jobs; their only means of earning money, to follow Him around the countryside, listening to Him teach and learn by watching what He did. In the process, they would learn how to teach people about God. Then, they would "fish" for people in order to bring people to a place where they understood how much God loves them.

ChallengePoint

Serving God begins with listening to Him and being willing to follow Him. That begins with people first hearing about God's love and that's where you come in – sharing the Good News. That's fishing for people!

Knowing God by
Serving Him

Just as each of us has one body with many members, and these members do not all have the same function, so in Christ we who are many form one body, and each member belongs to all the others.

✳ ROMANS 12:4-5

Do you play on a sports team? Think about a softball team as an example of how a team works. Each player on the team has a specific job – an area of the field to cover. If the ball is hit to the third base side of the field, the first baseman would not run across the field to grab the ball. Each player has a job to do and must not try to do someone else's job.

It's the same with God's body, of which you are a member. Some members of God's body have the job of teaching. Some have the job of encouraging others. Some are good at sharing their faith with others. You see, each person has a job to do for God, as part of His family.

ChallengePoint

There is probably something that you really enjoy doing and that you get a positive response from others about. That is a way you can serve God. Maybe you're good at making friends; listening to others, or teaching or sports or music. Whatever you're good at, you can serve God by doing that thing.

"You are the salt of the earth. But what good is salt if it has lost its flavor? Can you make it salty again? It will be thrown out and trampled underfoot as worthless."

✳ MATTHEW 5:13

If you dropped out of life you would hope that someone would notice, wouldn't you? You hope that your presence makes a difference to those around you and that they would notice if your influence was taken away. That means that you are like salt to those around you – you flavor their lives.

Why does Jesus use the example of salt in this verse? He's talking about Christians who are obeying God and serving Him; Christians who are taking a stand for Him. When a person stops doing that, then she isn't doing her job and her purpose is gone. God doesn't accept half-hearted obedience. He wants your full heart obeying Him all the time. Otherwise, you are like flavorless salt.

ChallengePoint

Do you want your life to count for something? Well, you know what to do … obey God. How terrible it would be to know that you've disappointed God by not obeying and serving Him. Then your purpose, your "saltiness" would be gone. It could happen … but it's up to you.

Knowing God by
Obeying Him

If we say we have not sinned, we make God a liar, and we do not accept God's teaching.

✳ 1 JOHN 1:10

There are some board games that are built around bluffing. In these games, you win by convincing the other players that what you claim to be true is true … even if it isn't. The weird thing is that if you are a convincing liar you can win the game.

This does not work in real life – at least not where God is concerned. You can't bluff with Him. You can't fool Him, so you might as well not even try. You can claim to other people that you don't do anything wrong. You can even give excuses about the choices you make and the things you do … but God knows the truth. He sees your heart and knows your motivations and selfishness. God insists on obedience and if you try to fake that obedience, you are just insulting Him.

ChallengePoint

Save yourself some heartache. Don't bother trying to fool God. Just be honest with Him. Come clean when you mess up – admit it and confess it. He wants your obedience, and He will forgive you when you confess. He loves you and will give you another chance to obey Him.

The world always looks brighter
from behind a smile.

~ ANONYMOUS

April

Knowing God by
Obeying Him

"What can a man give in exchange for his soul?"

✳ MARK 8:37

This question cuts through the junk in life. The bottom line of this answer will show you what is really the most important thing in your life. It's not an easy question to answer. Think about it. Really think about it.

What slides in front of your obedience to God? Friends? Popularity? Music? Sports? Be honest about this – no one has to know your answer but God and you. But know this – God doesn't mess around when it comes to obedience.

Being a child of God means obeying Him and that begins with asking Jesus to be your Savior. If anything else is more important to you than Him, then you will lose your soul and all chance of eternal life in heaven.

ChallengePoint

Look at the big picture of eternity with God. The right here and now will very quickly be the day that "used to be" and there are more important things. Don't give up your soul for what seems like a little bit of fun today.

Knowing God by
Obeying Him

Anyone who knows the right thing to do, but does not do it, is sinning.

* JAMES 4:17

Here's the situation: The most popular girl in your class decides she wants to be your friend. You start hanging out together at lunchtime, talking, giggling and sharing secrets. But then she decides to treat a girl of a different nationality in a rotten way. She makes fun of her, tells lies about her, makes her the subject of jokes, etc.

If you're going to stay friends with Miss Popular, then you're going to have to join in this behavior. You KNOW the right thing to do. Loving others is an important commandment to God. That doesn't involve making fun of other kids. Will you join Miss Popular in this?

If you do, you are totally and completely wrong. God says if you know the right thing to do and choose not to do it … it's sin. Plain and simple.

ChallengePoint

Obedience is very important to God. He doesn't mess around with it. Don't try to fake this – you may fool other people, but God knows. When you know deep in your heart that God disapproves of something and you do it anyway – it is sin.

Knowing God by
Confessing Sin

People who conceal their sins will not prosper, but if they confess and turn from them, they will receive mercy.

* PROVERBS 28:13

When you do something dumb it's always a temptation to try to hide it from others. No one wants others to know what a fool they've been. Well, you may be able to hide your foolishness from others, but you can't ever fool God.

That bears true in this verse. Things you choose to do in secret may truly be secret from other people – that is hidden sin – but not hidden from God. He knows about it. There are no secrets from Him. He always punishes sin.

That's how you learn to stop doing wrong things. There's only one way out of that punishment … confess your sins and God will forgive you.

ChallengePoint

Confession is cleansing. It cleans up your relationship with God. Your sin puts up a barrier between you and God. Confessing your sin tears it down and makes your relationship healthy again.

Knowing God by
Seeking His Guidance

All Scripture is God-breathed and is useful for teaching, rebuking, correcting and training in righteousness.

* 2 TIMOTHY 3:16

Do you spend a lot of time listening to music? Can you sing along to the lyrics of most of your favorite songs? You may even know all of your favorite groups' songs. That's cool. But, um, how many Bible verses do you know … by heart?

You've got an instruction book from God on how to live the Christian life. If you're going to do it right, it would help to read it. Not just read it, but memorize it so that it is buried in your heart and you can pull up a verse for whatever circumstance you're in.

ChallengePoint

The Bible teaches, corrects and trains. That covers everything you need to live the Christian life. If God's guidance and instruction comes from the Bible then it would make a lot of sense to read it, right? Yes. Read it and memorize it.

Knowing God by
Understanding Anger

Love isn't selfish or quick tempered. It doesn't keep a record of wrongs that others do.

* 1 CORINTHIANS 13:5

Love is pretty much the main theme of God's Word. There's a background to this verse. Here's how it goes:

- Jesus said loving others is the second most important command.
- 1 Corinthians 13 gives a description of how honest to goodness love acts.
- Loving others means not focusing on anger or insisting on always having its way.
- God guides His children away from anger and toward love.

ChallengePoint

Everyone gets angry sometimes, but if a person is focusing her heart on loving others (as God says to do), anger will not be the norm. Then when anger happens, it will go away quickly and be replaced by love.

Knowing God by
His Faithfulness

"Earth and sky will be destroyed, but the words I have said will never be destroyed."

* MARK 13:31

Laws change. Standards of what is right and what is wrong might change. But God's laws will never change. His Word, the Bible, will never change and never disappear. His words will live in the hearts of His children forever.

Do you believe that God's Words are forever? He says it's true. If you're not paying much attention to your Bible; if it's lying in the corner underneath a stack of magazines – then you're not living as though you believe God's Word is important. Faithfulness means forever, and God says His words will be around forever.

ChallengePoint

God's Word will last forever so you know it is important. It only makes sense to take time every day to read His Word and even memorize it. Think about it and let it settle in your mind and heart. It will guide your life.

Knowing God by
Seeking Salvation

Everyone who calls on the name of the LORD will be saved.

* JOEL 2:32

Have you ever gone through try-outs for a choir or a team? It can be a long process; lots of practices, then a series of try-outs with a cut after each one. Finding out if you've made the choir or the team may come down to standing in front a bulletin board, searching the list for your name.

Thankfully you don't have to go through that kind of process to become a member of God's family. God doesn't make you go through try-outs and cuts to join His family. All you have to do to be saved and become a member of God's family is … ask. God's plan is that Jesus came to earth, died for your sins, came back to life and now lives in heaven again with God, the Father. All you have to do is call on His name to be saved. Pretty easy, right?

ChallengePoint

God made the plan for salvation as easy as possible. Have you done it? Ask Jesus to live in your heart. Confess your sins and ask His forgiveness. You are then saved into His family.

Knowing God by
Being Thankful

Give thanks to the LORD, for He is good; His love endures forever.

* 1 CHRONICLES 16:34

Why does the Bible keep telling you to thank God for stuff? Does God really need your thanks? Well; no, He doesn't NEED it. But sure He enjoys being thanked – you do, too, right?

It's important, because when you take time to think about what you're thankful for, you're thinking about God. That helps your faith grow stronger because you realize how much He loves you and how many wonderful things He does for you. Saying thanks is so easy but doing it brings a lot of joy for you too.

ChallengePoint

Thankfulness helps you to get to know God better because as you think about what you are thankful for you understand God and all He does for you. What a happy thing. Take time every day to thank God for just one thing. Pretty soon, you won't be able to stop with just one thing!

Knowing God by
Celebrating Him

It is wonderful each morning to tell about Your love and at night to announce how faithful You are.

* PSALM 92:2

What's the first thing you think about when you wake up in the morning? What's for breakfast? Stuff you have to do that day? What you're going to wear?

How far down the list is "God loves me"? Then, what's your last thought before falling asleep at night? Probably something about what happened during the day. Do you end your day by remembering that God is faithful?

He keeps His promises, always and forever. He means what He says. He says what He means. He does what He says. He is faithful.

ChallengePoint

What a joy to start your day by remembering that God loves you no matter what. Then, what a peaceful thought to remember He is always faithful, just before you fall asleep. Those two things are worth celebrating. Throw a party! Sing a song! Celebrate how awesome God is!

Knowing God by
Enduring

And you, my son Solomon, acknowledge the God of your father, and serve Him with wholehearted devotion and with a willing mind, for the LORD searches every heart and understands every motive behind the thoughts. If you seek Him, He will be found by you; but if you forsake Him, He will reject you forever.

✳ 1 CHRONICLES 28:9

On a beautiful Saturday your mom loads you down with chores to do … inside chores. You want to be outside enjoying the nice day and doing something with your friends. So you kind of slosh your way through the chores as fast as possible and head out the door … until Mom checks on your work. You end up doing your half-hearted chores again! That stinks. Makes sense though. When you're doing a chore for Mom, give it everything. Do your best.

The same thing applies to knowing God. Search for God with everything you've got. That's endurance. It takes your whole heart and mind and it means you can't fake your way through. God knows the real you.

ChallengePoint

Give all your energy and strength to knowing God. Work hard, be strong, give it your all. It's worth it to know God with your whole heart and mind.

Knowing God by
Being Like Christ

"Do to others whatever you would like them to do to you. This is the essence of all that is taught in the law and the prophets."

* MATTHEW 7:12

This verse is the Golden Rule. Treat others the way you want to be treated. Pretty simple, right? If you tell lies about someone else then she can lie about you. Yeah, that's not fun, is it?

Living like Christ means treating others with respect, honesty and love. That's how you'd like to be treated, right? Amazingly, Christ even treated His enemies that way. He even understood how to disagree with others in a respectful way.

Christ put a lot of importance on treating others kindly. It's important to Him.

ChallengePoint

There's no denying that loving others is not always easy. Some people are so sold on themselves that no one wants to be around them. But it's a good reminder to treat others the way you would like to be treated. The first step to treating others the way Christ did is to treat them the way you would like to be treated yourself.

Being Like Christ

Do not be interested only in your own life, but be interested in the lives of others.

* PHILIPPIANS 2:4

This may come as a surprise to you, but life isn't all about you. In your mind, what happens with your friends, how your parents get along, whether your family has to move, if your dad loses a job … is only important in how it affects you or how it makes you look. But to live like Christ you have to make your brain think differently. It's Christlike to look at things and think about how other people are affected.

Think about how things make them feel. Then celebrate with them when they have good news (even if it's not good news for YOU) and sympathize with them when they have sad news (even if it's great news for you). Is this easy? Nope. Is it important? Yep.

ChallengePoint

Here's a tip – think about life with this kind of priority in mind: Jesus first, others next, you last. Put others' needs and concerns before your own.

Knowing God by
Loving Others

"Love your enemies! Do good to them. Lend to them without expecting to be repaid. Then your reward from heaven will be very great, and you will truly be acting as children of the Most High, for He is kind to those who are unthankful and wicked."

* LUKE 6:35

Are you a list-maker? Do you like to have a list of things that need to be accomplished so you can tick them off? Look at the list in this verse:

1. Love God. (OK, done. That's an easy one.)
2. Love others. (Done. After all, it's easy to love your friends.)
3. Love your enemies. (Whoa. Love your enemies? Right. NO WAY.)

Well, you must – if you're going to love the way God loves.

ChallengePoint

As you're struggling with this idea, think about this ... God loves those who are unthankful and wicked ... sometimes that means YOU. Now, aren't you glad He loves that way? Can you learn from Him and love that way too?

Knowing God by
Loving Others

Love is patient and kind. Love is not jealous, it does not brag, and it is not proud.

* 1 Corinthians 13:4

The way movies, TV shows and even songs portray love is a mushy kind of thing. But there's a lot more depth to love than you might understand. The thirteenth chapter of 1 Corinthians explains love. In fact, it defines love. It's really helpful to understand what love is and how it behaves since the Bible is filled with the command to love others.

This verse alone tells you two things love is: patient and kind. It also tells you three things love isn't: jealous, envious or proud. These are ways to measure your emotions about someone and you'll find out if you're really a loving person or not.

ChallengePoint

You are probably a very loving person. But remember that the command to love extends to people that are kind of hard to love too. It also includes brothers and sisters who are a pain sometimes. That's where patience and kindness need to come in. Loving others is really important to God. One Corinthians 13 is a place to begin to measure your emotions and see how you're doing in the "loving others" department.

Knowing God by
Showing Courage

So be strong and courageous! Do not be afraid and do not panic before them. For the LORD your God will personally go ahead of you. He will neither fail you nor abandon you.

✳ DEUTERONOMY 31:6

Some girls are "girly girls" who are afraid of pretty much everything from storms to spiders. Other girls are proud to say that not much of anything scares them. Wherever you fit in doesn't really matter. Even the bravest of girls is scared once in a while – whether she admits it or not.

Actually, sometimes the scariest thing you have to face is the feeling that you're alone. Feeling as though you have to figure things out by yourself and come up with a plan alone, or that you have to battle through a problem by yourself can be overwhelming. Take courage from this: YOU ARE NOT ALONE. God promised to stick close to you. Even better, He says He will go ahead of you.

ChallengePoint

Does it give you courage to know that God is always with you and that nothing surprises Him? He knows what's going to happen in your life before it happens. In fact, He's already got a plan laid out to deal with it. He will not fail you.

Knowing God by
Witnessing His Power

We can win with God's help. He will defeat our enemies.

* PSALM 60:12

When you choose teams in gym class and start a game, if you've got the biggest, strongest person in the class on your team, you are in good shape. No worries. Nothing to fear. Your team is bigger and more powerful than the other one so you are assured of a win.

You understand then how cool it is to be on God's team. His power will smash His enemies, who, by the way, are your enemies too. His amazing power is fighting for you, protecting you and guiding you!

ChallengePoint

Knowing that God is on your side and that His amazing power is fighting for you and protecting you should give you great peace. This doesn't mean that you won't be afraid sometimes. Of course you will. But tell God what's going on and then look for His power protecting and guiding you. If you get scared – remember how powerful He is!

Knowing God by
Having Faith

What good is it, dear brothers and sisters, if you say you have faith but don't show it by your actions? Can that kind of faith save anyone?

* JAMES 2:14

OK, you may know someone like this: she says one thing – all sweet, nice and supportive – but her actions do not back up what she says, she ignores people, pushes them aside, and tries to be important. This is called lip service. It is what you give when you say all the right things, but your actions don't back up what you say.

You can even do this with Christian things by saying all the right Christian words about loving and praying for others. You may know Bible verses and go to church every week, but if your life doesn't actually show love and concern for others, then all your Christian words are just a waste of good air. Faith is more than knowing how to say the right words. Faith shows in how you live – concern for others and a desire to love and help them.

ChallengePoint

Don't bother with lip service. It is a waste of time and doesn't fool God at all. Put your faith into action. Do the work God wants you to do. Don't just talk about it ... do it.

Giving

By everything I did, I showed how you should work to help every-one who is weak. Remember that our Lord Jesus said, "More bless-ings come from giving than from receiving."

* ACTS 20:35

This Scripture verse doesn't mean giving by just sharing your lunch with a friend or loaning someone your sweater because she left hers at home. Come on, you've seen pictures of kids in other parts of the world who don't even have food to eat. Some of them don't have homes and others live in mud huts. The idea of them owning video games, cell phones, TV's … ridiculous. People who don't know where their next meal is coming from don't worry about that kind of stuff.

So what should this mean to you? What God has given to you should be shared with those who have needs. Plain and simple.

ChallengePoint

You know, it feels good to help someone. Giving doesn't always mean giving money. As a kid you may not have a lot of money to give. Sometimes you can help others by giving time to help them with something. You can add your little bit of money to other money given by others through church, for example, to make a big difference to others.

Knowing God by
Suppressing Pride

"Why do you look at the speck of sawdust in your brother's eye and pay no attention to the plank in your own eye?"

* MATTHEW 7:3

Be honest about this – when a group of girls get together it is possible for the conversation to get a little snarkey – criticizing others, picking apart how someone dresses or her talents, her grades, her home. It can get ugly. It becomes a pride issue.

Pride blinds you to your own faults. Pride puffs you up like a blowfish to think you're pretty awesome and amazing. Pride pushes others down by focusing on their problems and faults. After all, it makes you feel better about yourself if you compare yourself to someone who is messing up or failing all the time.

Pride doesn't fool God. He says to take care of your own issues and not worry about others.

ChallengePoint

Criticizing others while ignoring your own problems is not in line to God's Word. Take care of your own problems. Ask God to help you focus on being more obedient to Him and more loving to others. Take care of yourself and let others take care of themselves.

Knowing God by
Abiding in Him

"Be still, and know that I am God! I will be honored by every nation. I will be honored throughout the world."

How often is your world quiet? Do you study best with music on in the background? Is your home noisy with brothers and sisters? School and friends bring talking and other kinds of noise. When is your world quiet and still so your mind can just relax?

Why is the quiet important? Because in the stillness you can more easily hear God's voice. It's hard to hear Him when there is clamor all around you. You've got to make this quiet time happen though.

It comes by being alone, turning off the tunes and just being still as you think about God and His Word. Try it.

ChallengePoint

This time with God is called "abiding." It means hanging out with God; being really close to Him; being quiet and listening for Him to speak in your heart. It's the way to know Him. Make time in your life to be in a quiet place, be still and think about God. Choose a verse or a phrase and just think about it for awhile. Enjoy just hanging out with God.

Knowing God by
Trusting Him

It is better to trust the LORD than to trust people.

* PSALM 118:8

No one is saying that good friends aren't important. They are. Friends are a gift from God. No one is saying that you should not have a friend to whom you can tell your secrets and share your thoughts. You should. It's healthy. But when it comes to choosing who you should trust more than anyone else in the world, it is important to keep things in perspective.

Friends are great, but they are human and once in a while they may let you down; even if they don't mean to. A refuge … a safe place to hide … needs to be a place where you will be safe … no matter what. God is the safest place. If you put trust in people instead of God, you will find that people fail sometimes. They make mistakes. They disappoint.

ChallengePoint

Friends are great and will be as loyal as they can. But things change, people change and friendships change. God is always the same. He is strong, powerful and loves you more than you can imagine. Putting your trust in Him is the safest and best choice. You can always count on God.

Knowing God by
Using His Gifts

I sing to the LORD because He has taken care of me.

＊ PSALM 13:6

How do you praise God? What's your favorite way? Some people sing at the top of their lungs – some good and some not. Some people love to wander through the woods and marvel at God's creation. Some people enjoy writing, others like to cook, some play sports, some are good at visiting people.

God gives everyone talents and abilities and He loves it when they use those things to serve and praise Him.

Don't get hung on whether you are the "best" at whatever you do. That doesn't matter. Just do what you can with joy and praise in your heart to God who made it all possible.

ChallengePoint

Sing, dance, write, be a friend, be a helper ... gifts and abilities come in lots of different forms. Recognize what you're good at and use it to serve God! It's the gift He gave you, so give it back to Him.

Knowing God by
His Love

But the LORD said to Samuel, "Don't look at how handsome Eliab is or how tall he is, because I have not chosen him. God does not see the same way people see. People look at the outside of a person, but the LORD looks at the heart."

* 1 SAMUEL 16:7

The media puts so much importance on outward appearance! Wow, if you're skinny, with great skin, good clothes, nice hair, you've got it made! Good looking means success!

That's dumb. God doesn't care what a person looks like on the outside. He judges a person's worth by what's going on in her heart. If her heart is focused on serving God, then she is a success in God's eyes. Outer beauty doesn't matter at all.

ChallengePoint

Girls spend a lot of time working on their outer appearance. But God's love focuses on your heart. How is your heart doing? Does it want to serve Him? Does it love God? Is God the most important Person in your life? He loves you lots and He doesn't get hung up on how you look, like people do. God just loves you. Pretty cool, huh?

Knowing God by
Praying

If any of you need wisdom, you should ask God, and it will be given to you. God is generous and won't correct you for asking.

* JAMES 1:5

Who is your "go-to" person when you need advice? Hopefully, it is someone trustworthy and mature. The best person to ask for advice is God. He is always ready to listen and always ready to answer. He never gets annoyed at your requests.

This doesn't mean that He will always do what you ask Him to do or change what you want changed. That's because He knows what's best for you. But He will always listen and He will advise you, if you're willing to listen to Him.

ChallengePoint

To hear God's advice, you must be quiet and let Him speak in your mind or heart. You can also read His Word and let Him speak to you through verses that you read. God sees the big picture of your whole life and the lives of those around you. He will hear your requests and prayers. He may not do what you think He should, but He does what's best for you in the long run. Ask Him whatever you want, tell Him your requests. Trust His answer.

Knowing God by
Seeking His Protection

The LORD gives His people strength. The LORD blesses them with peace.

* PSALM 29:11

Sticks and stones may break my bones but words will never harm me." Have you heard that little saying before? Yeah, it's not true. Words always hurt. So how does God protect you from mean, abusive words?

Sometimes the protection He gives you comes from inside you. He makes you strong enough to stand up to abuse. He helps you fight against temptation. He gives you peace when it seems like there is chaos all around you. He helps you be the person you've always been capable of being even if you didn't know it.

ChallengePoint

Wow, it's cool to think that God sometimes protects you by working in your heart to help you be a stronger person. That means He is helping you grow up to be an amazing woman of God.

Knowing God by
Seeking His Protection

I find true comfort, LORD, because Your laws have stood the test of time.

* PSALM 119:52

Some girls follow every rule down to the tiniest point. Others have so much trouble with rules that they are constantly stretching them and pushing the limits. You need to remember that rules are actually there to protect you. Hopefully, they keep you from doing dumb things or making bad choices.

Rules also help make life more pleasant for everyone. Rules keep you safe from dangers of all kinds. God's laws are rules to live by. There's no denying that His commands are hard to keep sometimes, but they do give you guidelines to know right from wrong. In the long run that makes life easier.

ChallengePoint

Remember that God gives laws and commands because He loves you. He wants you to be safe. He wants to help you learn to be a stronger Christian and a better person. It's a little easier to accept rules when you think of God's laws like that.

Knowing God by
Serving Him

Two people are better than one, because they get more done by working together.

* ECCLESIASTES 4:9

What an awesome understanding of people God has. Duh … He created them so He should understand them. He knew that life is easier if you're not all by yourself. Friends have different skills and gifts and can compliment other friends. So, what you are good at, your friend may not be so good at, and vice versa. You need each other!

This verse encourages teamwork and friendship. There is strength in numbers. Friends can encourage you to be the best person you can be. They pick you up when you stumble. They cover for you when you're down. Now, here's some great news … you're on God's team. He does all those things for you too.

ChallengePoint

Even serving God can be lonely sometimes. But the realization that part of serving Him means you are on His team is an encouragement. Look around at the people God has placed in your life who are your friends. God put them there to help and encourage you and for you to do the same for them!

Knowing God by
Serving Him

"He must become greater; I must become less."

✳ JOHN 3:30

Some people are terrified of public speaking. Are you one of those people? Are you way more comfortable being behind-the-scenes? Do you enjoy being a supporter who helps the girls out front look good? That probably means that the out-front people are the ones who will get the attention and praise. Are you OK with that?

Put that thought on hold for a minute and think about this: Does it kind of seem like a no-brainer to say that serving God is important? So are you willing to become more and more of a background person as you serve Him so that He becomes more and more important? That means that the work you do points people to Him. So instead of them praising your abilities (Wow, you're an awesome singer) they will praise God.

ChallengePoint

As God becomes Number One, your desires and needs will kind of fade to the background. You'll be more and more eager to do what He wants and to serve Him in anyway you can. And ... amazingly ... you'll be more filled with joy than ever before!

Knowing God by
Obeying Him

"No one can serve two masters. For you will hate one and love the other; you will be devoted to one and despise the other. You cannot serve both God and money."

✳ MATTHEW 6:24

OK, girl, you have to make a choice. See, that's one of the cool things about God – He lets you choose to obey Him … or not. He doesn't make you do anything. But you have to make a choice. It doesn't work to say you are a God-follower on Sunday, but live like a stinker on Tuesday.

Either you're on God's team or you're not. If you try to ride the fence and be "on God's team" today but do your own thing tomorrow, you will end up not being on any team. God won't accept half of your heart. He insists on full-service followers.

❊ ChallengePoint

Trying to "serve two masters" never works. You can't fool God. Remember, He sees your heart so He knows where your loyalty is. Don't try to serve God and something else. Give God your whole heart.

Knowing God by
Obeying Him

Be on your guard and stay awake. Your enemy, the devil, is like a roaring lion, sneaking around to find someone to attack.

* 1 PETER 5:8

Video games are a lot of fun. In most games, you try to get from Point A to Point B so you can move up to the next level. The conflict is that there is a bad guy or a barrier always trying to trip you up and make you fail. It makes the game more challenging and fun. It takes practice and skill to overcome the obstacles.

Did you know that in real life the devil constantly tries to trip you up and keep you from obeying God? That's not fun. The devil is sneaky and he disguises himself as beautiful things like fame or success. God warns you about the devil. He knows what a creep the devil is.

ChallengePoint

You have to pay attention and stay alert because the devil will do everything in his power to keep you from obeying God. He is relentless. He wants you on his team, but you can't be on his and on God's. Thank goodness God will help you. He wants your obedience so He will help you fight off Satan's attacks. God never leaves you to fight alone. If obeying God is very important to you, ask Him for help. He will be there for you.

You are a gift to the world, a divine work of art, signed by God.

~ MAX LUCADO

May

Knowing God by
His Forgiveness

"Come back to Me, you unfaithful children, and I will forgive you for being unfaithful." Yes, we will come to You, because You are the Lord our God.

∗ JEREMIAH 3:22

Oh man, you messed up again. It seems like every time you open your mouth, the wrong thing comes out. You don't mean to keep doing it. It just seems to happen. So, you're forever asking your friends or family to forgive you. Aren't you glad when they do? Forgiveness is modeled by God. He promises to forgive you when you mess up and come asking for His forgiveness. The thing is, God wants to forgive you.

However, forgiveness requires something from you. God asks you to choose to come back to Him; choose to ask His forgiveness. That's not hard when you recognize who God is and how much He loves you.

ChallengePoint

The hardest part is admitting when you've messed up or disobeyed. It's hard to admit failure. But the amazing gift of forgiveness from Almighty God is worth it. So, it only makes sense to accept it. God doesn't require much from you. He just wants you to come to Him. That's not hard. It means admitting your failures and asking Him for help. You can do it!

Knowing God by
Seeking Guidance

He gives me new strength. He leads me on paths that are right for the good of His name.

* PSALM 23:3

Do you need a GPS in your soul? You know what a GPS is, right? It's those thingies that talk to you in the car and tell you "Turn left. Drive 1 mile and turn right." You enter the address of your destination and it tells you how to get there.

Guess what, you actually have a kind of GPS inside of you – God! Yeah, He will guide you in how to live a righteous life; a life of obedience to Him. Does that amaze you? It's true. Talk to Him and read His Word and your GPS by God will kick in!

ChallengePoint

It's true that God will guide your life. He has a plan for your life. That may sound amazing – the God of creation cares about little old you. But He does and He will give you strength to keep growing and learning.

Knowing God by
His Faithfulness

Surely Your goodness and love will be with me all my life, and I will live in the house of the LORD forever.

* PSALM 23:6

This is how it works when you grow up and move out of your parents' house. Typically, you find an apartment to rent and you get a job to earn money to pay the rent. That's cool, until one month you spend too much money on clothes and you can't pay your rent. Then the next month you decide to eat out every meal and you have no money left for rent. Do you know what happens then? You get evicted – kicked out of your home! That would stink.

You never have to worry about that with God, though. Some day you will live in His house just as this verse says. You can count on that being FOREVER. He pursues you with love and kindness. That means He's running after you, calling you to come to Him!

ChallengePoint

Why does God pursue you? Because He loves you! He wants to fill your life with His goodness and His love. He wants to bless you. So, stop running right now and look around you. God is there. Spend some time with Him!

Knowing God by
Seeking Salvation

Everyone has sinned; we all fall short of God's glorious standard.

✻ ROMANS 3:23

Oh, young friend, be careful how critical you are of other people. It's such a temptation to point out others' sins – even to God. But never ignore the fact that you're on the same plane as those you're criticizing.

Here are the facts: God created people in His image. That means people were perfect. The first people sinned by disobeying God. That changed all people for the rest of time from perfect to broken – all people are sinners.

God sent Jesus to earth to die for the sins of all people so that people can come to heaven. That means Jesus died for you.

Why did God come up with this plan? Simple … 'cause He loves you.

ChallengePoint

You can try to convince yourself that you never do anything wrong … but you'll never convince God because He knows your hidden thoughts and any secret things you do. Everyone sins. But because of God's amazing love for you, He came up with a plan to help you. That's the plan of salvation.

Knowing God by
Being Thankful

Continue praying, keeping alert, and always thanking God.

✳ COLOSSIANS 4:2

When you've gone out of your way to do something kind for someone, it is nice to be thanked. Especially if the person you've been kind to is constantly, repeatedly asking for things. That's why God instructs you to be thankful in the middle of your praying. Don't get so caught up in the asking that you don't even notice what He is doing for you.

He's not some big Santa Claus in the sky that you can just shoot request after request to with no understanding of what your relationship is. HE LOVES YOU. That's why He answers your prayers and takes care of you. So, in the midst of your constant prayers, pay attention to the answers … and thank Him for them.

ChallengePoint

God does more for you than anyone else ever could. Pay attention to His care and His acts of love and thank Him.

Knowing God by
Celebrating Him

Shout for joy to the LORD, all the earth, burst into jubilant song with music; make music to the LORD with the harp, with the harp and the sound of singing, with trumpets and the blast of the ram's horn – shout for joy before the LORD, the King.

✽ PSALM 98:4-6

What makes you and your friends really celebrate? What makes you stand up and shout and then jump up and down with excitement?

Have you ever celebrated God that way? Why not? Sometimes worship is so sedate that it's hard to find any joy in it at all. God wants you to celebrate. He is awesome and He loves you very much.

He wants you to notice all the ways He shows that love and all the care He gives you. If you take time to celebrate Him, you will be taking time to actually name the things to celebrate.

ChallengePoint

Naming things to celebrate means that you are taking notice of all God does in this world and all He does for you every day. There is so much to celebrate that you will need to do a happy dance every day!

Knowing God by
Enduring

I focus on this one thing: Forgetting the past and looking forward to what lies ahead, I press on to reach the end of the race and receive the heavenly prize for which God, through Christ Jesus, is calling us.

✳ PHILIPPIANS 3:13-14

Long-distance runners seldom look like they are having fun. Have you ever seen a runner on TV who is smiling? Why do runners keep running? The answer is: the joy of finishing what they start. Running is a sport of endurance. The runner has to keep going, through pain, bad weather, discouragement and loneliness.

It is actually good training for life. Life is going to be hard sometimes. There's not much you can do about it. But things that are worthwhile take a lot of work. That's just the way it is. But when you have problems or when bad things happen, remember, you aren't out on the road by yourself – ask God for strength to get through it.

ChallengePoint

If you quit trying just because things get hard, you'll never grow stronger as a Christian. There is also the danger of developing the habit of not finishing things you start. That's not good. God wants to help you learn and grow. He will give you endurance to get through the tough things. Just ask Him.

Knowing God by
Enduring

Training your body helps you in some ways, but serving God helps you in every way by bringing you blessings in this life and in the future life, too.

* 1 TIMOTHY 4:8

You can get psycho about taking care of your body. There is so much importance put on body image these days that some girls sink into eating disorders because they never believe they are thin enough. Of course it's a good idea to take care of your body, but don't go overboard on that. Remember to be healthy.

In all your body training, don't forget your heart and soul. That means, don't forget the part of you that is constantly learning to know God better. Your heart obeys God and as it is "trained" you learn to love others the way God does. You learn to lean on Him through problems. You learn to endure whatever life throws your way.

ChallengePoint

No training of any kind is easy. In fact, it's work. Training in godliness is no different because it's such an up-and-down thing – dependent on your obedience and submission to God. But the benefits are amazing – a strong soul as you become more and more like God. Train your body, but don't forget to train for godliness too!

Knowing God by
Being Like Christ

"The seeds that fell on good ground are the people who hear and understand the message. They produce as much as a hundred or sixty or thirty times what was planted."

* MATTHEW 13:23

Dirt is dirt, right? Wrong. A wise gardener would not just go out and toss seeds around without checking out the soil. If it's too rocky or too shallow or has a lot of weeds in it, your gardening efforts will not be successful. But if you plant seeds in healthy soil with good drainage and good minerals in it, you will grow healthy plants.

God says to think about your heart in that way too. If God's Word is spoken to you or if you read it, then it lands in your heart. A healthy heart will let that seed settle in and begin to grow. There won't be rocks of disobedience or weeds of resentment that block its growth. When it grows your heart becomes more and more like Christ: kind, loving and obedient.

ChallengePoint

How do you get a healthy heart? That starts with giving your heart to Christ. It stays healthy by talking with Him in prayer and asking Him to help you be obedient to Him. It's a series of choices every day to go God's way, not your own.

Knowing God by
Being Like Christ

Think about the things that are good and worthy of praise. Think about the things that are true and honorable and right and pure and beautiful and respected.

✳ PHILIPPIANS 4:8

The girls you hang out with and the things you talk about is the food you are putting in your mind. If you put garbage in, garbage will come out. So, if you take part in gossiping about others, if you watch junk on TV, if you go to Internet sites that you know you shouldn't visit … the attitudes and actions you pick up will eventually show up in your life. That's because you get used to them and they don't seem so bad.

If you want your life to be like Christ's life, then fill your mind with things that are like Him. Read books or watch programs that have good messages. Spend time with people who model kindness and love. Put good stuff in and good stuff will come out in the way you live.

ChallengePoint

Does that mean you can't watch TV or play video games? No, it just means to be careful what kinds of messages you bombard your mind with. Does it mean you can't hang out with some friends? Maybe. Choose things that are honoring to God and that will remind you to be like Christ.

Knowing God by
Being Like Christ

When you are with unbelievers, always make good use of the time. Be pleasant and hold their interest when you speak the message. Choose your words carefully and be ready to give answers to anyone who asks questions.

* COLOSSIANS 4:5-6

You've probably been around a person who pretends to be interested in you, but you can tell by the way she looks at you and responds to you that she is just sizing you up and probably even judging you as she talks with you. Don't do that. Remember that people are watching you. All the time. Every word you say. Every thing you do. Every attitude you show.

These things show your opinion of the person you are talking to, and even more important, your opinion of God. They show how important He truly is to you. That's why you're told to be smart about your actions and words, especially with those who don't know Christ. That's what God wants you to do.

ChallengePoint

It's scary to think that people are watching you to see what God is like. It's a reminder that your basic purpose for being on this planet is to share God's love with others. Make your words and actions count for Christ.

Being Like Christ

Suppose someone has enough to live and sees a brother or sister in need, but does not help. Then God's love is not living in that person.

* 1 John 3:17

Do you have a tender heart? Sometimes it is heart-breaking to see how others live and to know that there are a lot of hungry people in this world. No doubt, some live in your town. Some live across the country. Some live in other countries. So what? So … God says to help them.

It's good that your heart hurts for people in need, but it isn't enough. Jesus said that the second most important command (second only to loving God) is to love others. If you love others, then when you see them hurting, you will do whatever you can to help. Christ certainly did. When He saw people who needed something – whether it was food or healing – He took care of the problem.

ChallengePoint

What can you do? You may not have money to give, but you can volunteer time in a food pantry or a place where meals are served to the poor. You can research what the needs are in your town, then make sure people know about those needs. See what programs your church has for helping others and get involved in any way you can. Be like Christ by loving others.

Knowing God by
Loving Others

Finally, all of you, live in harmony with one another; be sympathetic, love as brothers, be compassionate and humble.

* 1 PETER 3:8

Ha! God wouldn't tell you to love others as brothers if He knew YOUR brother, right? This Scripture verse tells you to get along with others and care about their feelings. Then it says to treat them like brothers. Seems like a conflict, doesn't it? OK, it's a known fact that brothers and sisters disagree and, yes, even argue and fight. HOWEVER, when push comes to shove and someone else starts picking on your brother, you would probably be the first to step up and defend him.

As you get older you'll probably get along with your brothers and sisters better. You will love them the way God says – with a tender and humble attitude.

ChallengePoint

God wants His children to get along. OK, sometimes that isn't easy, but it can be done with God's help. God wants His children to stand out from the world by the love they show one another. Do you need help with that? God is complete love and He will share that love with you.

Knowing God by
Showing Courage

If we endure hardship, we will reign with Him. If we deny Him, He will deny us.

✷ 2 TIMOTHY 2:12

You may have a "friend" who is buddy-buddy with you when it's convenient, but when someone else decides you aren't cool, then she takes off running. She doesn't stand up for you – that's not a real friend. That's the way friendship with God is too. Only you're the one who might do the running.

It's when the stuff of life gets tough that you find out how real your faith in God is. It is easy to claim you trust God when everything is going smoothly. But when things get tough, then you find out whether you really do trust God. If you get so mad at God when problems come that you run away, then your faith wasn't very strong to begin with. He wants your faith to be real so that you courageously face whatever hard things happen.

ChallengePoint

If your faith in God is real then His strength will give you courage to handle life as it comes. Some things in life are painful. It's OK to hurt or to be sad. It's even OK to be angry … for a while. But God's strength will help you handle these hard things. Trust Him and your courage will grow!

Knowing God by
Witnessing His Power

It is by faith we understand that the whole world was made by God's command so what we see was made by something that cannot be seen.

* HEBREWS 11:3

Can you imagine making something out of nothing? God did. He just spoke the words and BAM – the whole world came into existence.

Look up at the night-time sky and you see a bazillion stars. God made them. Stand at the base of a mountain so high that its peaks are lost in the clouds. God made it. Look at the ocean so wide and deep that you can't imagine the actual size of it. God made it. Think of the giant redwood trees. A single tree is big enough to cut a hole through so that a car can drive through it. God made them. Think about waterfalls so big and powerful that electricity is powered by them. God made them. The flaming hot sun, the moon that controls the tides … God made them all.

God's power is seen everywhere in nature. Everything was made by Him … from nothing!

ChallengePoint

God's power as revealed in nature is truly amazing. He made everything from scratch! What's even more amazing is that, as His child, that power is available to help and guide you in life.

Knowing God by
Trusting Him

But the LORD has chosen you to be His own people. He will always take care of you so that everyone will know how great He is.

✴ 1 SAMUEL 12:22

Belonging to a group or a team is awesome. It feels so good to belong to something. Some kids go over the top though and trust no one except those who are in their group or club. That's a problem if those they trust do not have their best interests in mind. They may let down the girl who trusts them to take care of her.

Hopefully you know people you can trust; people who will stand up for you and be there for you no matter what. Your family is probably in that category and hopefully some friends too. Have you thought about this though?

The best person for you to trust is God. He promises to stick with you, guide you, protect you and just LOVE you. That will never change … He promises.

ChallengePoint

Even dependable and trustworthy people may sometimes disappoint you. Sometimes their own feelings get in the way of promises to support you. Remember that God doesn't change. He does not break His promises. He never changes. You can always count on Him.

Knowing God by
His Love

The LORD is kind and shows mercy. He does not become angry quickly but is full of love.

✳ PSALM 145:8

People are victims of moods. You know how it is. Something happens and your mood swings from high to low, happy to crabby, encouraging to critical. Even someone who loves you can be difficult because of the mood she is in.

You don't have to worry about that where God is concerned. He is not a victim of moods. He doesn't get angry and blow up at you. He is always loving and always kind. His constant, unfailing love for you wants you to succeed. He wants the best for you. That means He is willing to forgive you when you fail. It means He is patient with you. He cares about you and will give you chance after chance to obey Him. There is nothing else on earth to compare to God's love.

ChallengePoint

It's nice to not need to worry about God's moods, isn't it? Read this verse again and think about what it means to you. God loves you very much. That love shows in His patience, forgiveness and steadiness. He wants the best for you. Does His amazing love for you make you love Him more?

Knowing God by
Praying

Listen to my voice in the morning, LORD. Each morning I bring my requests to You and wait expectantly.

* PSALM 5:3

How do your days start? Do you leap up with a smile on your face as soon as the alarm sounds? The psalmist thought it was a good idea to start each day by talking to God. God must think that's a good idea, too, since this verse is in the Bible.

Why would He think that? Simple. What better way to start your day than by focusing your thoughts on God, by asking Him to help you obey Him and serve Him throughout the day. God wants to be part of your whole day.

ChallengePoint

God wants to be part of your whole day because He loves you. If you start your day by talking with Him, then you will think about Him throughout the day. You can ask Him to help you make good choices. He will listen as you explain the things that concern you and then He will take care of them. He does all of this because He loves you.

Knowing God by
Seeking His Protection

The LORD defends those who suffer; He defends them in times of trouble.

* PSALM 9:9

Do you have a "secret place" where you go to think things through? Some people have a hiding place in their house, their own room, up in a tree, a place in a park … some spot that is "theirs." When you're afraid, or just need to think things through, do you go to that place?

You see, everyone is afraid of something, whether they admit it or not, and people hide in different ways. Some hide by being mean to others; some hide by acting tough; by losing themselves in a hobby or a talent like sports.

However, the best place to go for protection when you're scared or in trouble: God. He's got the power over everything so He's the safest hiding place.

ChallengePoint

Have you ever thought about "hiding" in God? How do you do that? You hide in God by studying His Word so you know what His promises to you are. You hide in Him by talking to Him every day and telling Him how you're feeling. You hide in Him by learning to trust Him to take care of you.

Knowing God by
Serving Him

"What will you gain, if you own the whole world but destroy yourself?"

* MARK 8:36

What does it mean to be successful? To some it means being super-thin and having expensive clothes. To others it means a powerful career or fame. It takes a lot of time and energy to achieve that.

It's OK to be successful, but be careful not to lose your relationship with God as you're climbing to success. You could end up with all the money, power and fame in the world, but if you don't know God, you have nothing. Know why? Because one day everyone dies. Everyone. Eternity is what's ahead and if you don't know God you spend forever in hell … not fun.

ChallengePoint

Serving God means using the talents and abilities He gives you in the way He wants. It may take you to the top of your career. You may even become famous and earn lots of money – but that's not your ultimate goal. Serving God and pleasing Him is your goal.

Knowing God by
Serving Him

In His grace, God has given us different gifts for doing certain things well. So if God has given you the ability to prophesy, speak out with as much faith as God has given you.

* ROMANS 12:6

Do you read this verse and think, "Yeah right, like God has given me some special gift!" Do you feel just barely average, if that? It's no fun to feel that you aren't good at something. Everyone wants to be recognized as being good – at least at one thing.

You may not know what your "thing" is yet, but you are good at something. God gives each of His children some special gift. As your faith in Him grows strong and you learn to obey Him and follow Him, that "thing" will become evident. Once you know what your gift is, use it for Him.

ChallengePoint

Some people know their gift at a very young age. Others see it develop as they mature. Some gifts are obvious, like prophesying, preaching or healing. Some are quieter gifts like the ability to be a constant, caring friend. Gifts from God are things you enjoy doing for Him and for others. When you know what your gift is, use it for Him and for others with joy!

Knowing God by
Serving Him

Don't let anyone make fun of you, just because you are young. Set an example for other followers by what you say and do, as well as by your love, faith, and purity.

* 1 TIMOTHY 4:12

You want to be treated with more respect, be allowed to do grown-up things? Yeah, most young people do. It's frustrating to be treated like a kid all the time when you think you deserve more. You could end up feeling as though life is on hold and what you're doing right now is just kid stuff.

This Scripture verse shows that's not true. God doesn't waste a minute of your time. You can serve Him right now. The way you live – treating others with kindness and respect, being helpful, being humble, being honest – is an example to others of who God is.

ChallengePoint

Cool! One way you can be grown up right now is to live for God NOW. That shows others that you love God. When other kids your age see you living for God, that may have more impact on them than anything that a grown up could say or do. You can serve God right now, just by the way you live.

Knowing God by
Obeying Him

How can a young person stay pure? By obeying Your word.

✳ PSALM 119:9

Rules, rules, rules. No one likes rules. Whose rules do you follow? Everyone has rules. Don't think that once you're grown up you won't have to deal with rules, because that just isn't true. Grown ups have rules too – laws of the land, rules at work and God's rules on how to live and how to treat others.

There are some good things about rules. They give you guidelines to live by. That's what God's Word does. If you know what He says in His Word then you know what's expected of you and when you're disobeying Him. You will also know of His forgiveness and love. Everyone messes up sometimes. Although that doesn't make it OK, God constantly forgives, loves and teaches you to do better the next time.

❋ ChallengePoint

God's Word helps you to learn about obeying Him. Now, disobeying doesn't mean God turns His back on you. He will help you learn from your mistakes. He gave you the Bible to help you learn. It is His Words of guidance and instruction. Read it and learn.

Knowing God by
Obeying Him

But Jesus said, "No, blessed are those who hear the teaching of God and obey it."

* LUKE 11:28

It is so frustrating to try to talk to someone who can't hear very well or who simply has selective hearing – she's only listening when she wants to. You never know if the information you are trying to convey is understood by that person.

Wow, imagine how God must feel sometimes. He doesn't know if His info has gotten through to you. You may HEAR His Words, but do you KEEP them? Do you obey Him? The laws God put in place and wants you to obey will protect you and help you. They will help you get along with other people, which will mean that you, and the people around you, enjoy life more. God's laws are for your own good. Is it hard to obey all the time? Yes. Is it worth it? Yes.

ChallengePoint

It isn't easy to always obey. But when you stop resisting obedience and realize that God's laws protect you from bad choices that could totally mess up your life and guide you in how to treat other people, well, obeying is a lot easier. Hear God's Word and keep it!

Knowing God by
Obeying Him

Children, obey your parents in the Lord, for this is right.

✳ EPHESIANS 6:1

God wouldn't say this if He knew how difficult my parents are!" "Come on, they aren't fair to me so why should I obey them?" Do either of these comments sound familiar to you? God cares whether you obey your parents. Why? Because they are responsible to Him for teaching you and raising you to be a responsible adult. One of their responsibilities is to teach you about God and make you familiar with His Word. It is a big responsibility for them and it is a lot more work when a child is rebellious.

Obeying your parents is really for your own good. There may be times when it doesn't seem like it, but if you think about the big picture of your whole life, you will see that obeying them teaches you a lot. You learn how to obey so that you can then cooperate with a boss or on a team. Obedience is important.

ChallengePoint

Obeying your parents honors God. It follows the path He put in place which leads to obeying Him. Everyone has trouble obeying sometimes, but make every effort to learn from your mistakes and obey more each day. It honors God and it honors your parents.

Knowing God by
Obeying Him

Don't you know that you are slaves of anyone you obey? You can be slaves of sin and die, or you can be obedient slaves of God and be acceptable to Him.

✳ ROMANS 6:16

Oh yeah, you want your freedom! You don't want to have to obey anyone! You want to be your own person! Stubbornly rebelling against God by refusing to obey His laws does not mean you are free. Sorry if you thought it did. The truth is that you belong to something or someone by what you choose to be a slave to.

If you choose to hang out with a group who doesn't care a bit about God and do the things they do, then you become a slave to that kind of life and your heart belongs to sin. Complete freedom doesn't exist – you always belong to something. God encourages you to belong to Him because that leads to eternal life in heaven. It's a good thing.

ChallengePoint

You can spout all you want about your freedom. The fact is, you belong to something – not to choose God is to choose something else. God encourages obedience to Him because in the big picture of life it is the best thing for you. Focus your heart on Him and make every effort to obey Him.

Knowing God by
Seeking His Guidance

LORD, since I have many enemies, show me the right thing to do. Show me clearly how You want me to live.

✳ PSALM 5:8

Sometimes it is hard to know the right thing to do. When you have enemies, you want to strike out at them and just hurt them. How do you know the right thing to do? You need a guide. A guide who has your best interests in mind and will be careful about where He leads you.

You don't have to worry about God as He guides your life. He wants to guide you and He wants you to succeed. Sometimes it may seem like He is hiding His instructions because you can't figure out what He wants from you. But more than likely, you're not putting yourself in a place where you can recognize His guidance.

ChallengePoint

God wants to guide your life. You know that because He gave you the Bible that is filled with His words and His values. He will also speak to your heart if you ask for His guidance, stay quiet, and listen to what He says.

Knowing God by
His Faithfulness

Give your burdens to the LORD, and He will take care of you. He will not permit the godly to slip and fall.

* PSALM 55:22

Some burdens are visible, like when you're carrying boxes of books. Some burdens are inside and no one knows about them except you and God. Some of the things you carry around in your heart get pretty heavy, don't they? Grief, guilt, worry and other emotions weigh you down.

Guess what? You can get rid of them. God wants to take them off your back and help you. How does He do it? He fills you with His love and encouragement. He reminds you of your worth to Him. You can always count on Him, too, because He is faithful – He will always do what He says He will do.

ChallengePoint

OK, so exactly how do you give your burdens to God? It's not easy to stop worrying or grieving. You have to continually ask God to take the worry or grief away. Ask Him to take care of the situations and when the worry or grief pops back into your mind, just remind yourself that God is taking care of it and that you can trust Him to do so.

Knowing God by
Seeking Salvation

I mean that you have been saved by grace through believing. You did not save yourselves; it was a gift from God. It was not the result of your own efforts, so you cannot brag about it.

✳ EPHESIANS 2:8-9

A gift – something that is given to you. You don't earn it. You don't deserve it. You don't buy it. It is a gift, plain and simple. Salvation is a gift to you from God. He gives you the chance to accept His gift of salvation from your sin and the future of forever being separated from Him just because He loves you.

Yep, He loves you and really wants you to be a part of His family. Grace is the reason – grace means that He gives this gift even though you don't deserve it (no one does) and you've done nothing to earn it. He forgives your sins, loves you, saves you, all because of His grace.

ChallengePoint

This is the most wonderful gift that will ever be given to you. By definition though, a gift is only a gift if you accept it. Have you accepted God's gift of salvation? That means admitting your sin, confessing it, and asking forgiveness as you ask Jesus to come into your heart and be your Savior. It's a gift because of God's amazing love for you.

When you have many kinds of troubles, you should be full of joy.

✳ JAMES 1:2

Celebrate your problems! R-i-i-i-g-g-h-h-t-t! Bring on the problems. Give me more! Is that what this verse means? Not exactly. Why should you consider trouble something to celebrate? Because of what you can learn from trouble:

1. You learn to trust God because He will get you through the problem.
2. You learn that there is strength inside you that you never knew you had.
3. Your faith will grow stronger as you see that God is helping you.

ChallengePoint

It's a little easier to make it through problems if you can see a purpose to them. Endurance is when you keep on plodding through problems and difficulties. That's a whole lot easier to do when you know God is working on things for you. When you have problems, go to Him right away and see what happens and what you can learn!

Knowing God by
Being Like Christ

A gentle answer deflects anger, but harsh words make tempers flare.

* PROVERBS 15:1

Anger brings out more anger, right? Who can respond to someone's anger with a gentle answer? Well, you've heard about WWJD … What Would Jesus Do? Have you thought about WWJS … What Would Jesus Say?

A gentle answer does not mean being a meek, quiet thing who can be walked all over. Jesus wasn't a wimp when He walked on this earth. When someone was messing up and needed to be told, He told them … but His words were always couched with love and concern for those around Him. If one man was teaching or doing things that were going to hurt someone else, Jesus set him straight. Jesus didn't respond with angry words. He was straightforward but respectful. There's a lesson there.

ChallengePoint

When someone gets angry with you and shouts angry words, how do you respond? If you get angry and shout back then the things will get worse and a relationship will be damaged that doesn't have to be. You can slow things down with a gentle response. That doesn't mean you have to take abuse, it means you don't respond with abuse. Gentle is better.

A cheerful heart brings a smile to your face.

~ Proverbs 15:13

June

Knowing God by
Being Like Christ

"Do not judge, or you too will be judged."

* MATTHEW 7:1

Judging others happens without you really thinking about it. A bunch of friends are sitting around talking, someone's name is mentioned and you start talking about her, and suddenly you're making judgments about her. You make judgments about other people all the time and sometimes it's just not fair.

How do you feel when someone decides that you're dumb, unkind, not athletic, dishonest? Being judged by people who don't really know you is no fun. It's not fair, either. Jesus taught that judging others leads to being judged yourself – by God. When He met people He gave them a chance to prove themselves. Remember? He talked to hated tax collectors and women – people that the important members of society ignored. Some of those people became powerful leaders of the church.

ChallengePoint

You don't like to be judged, so don't make judgments of others. When you judge someone as not being "good" enough to be your friend, you might miss getting to know someone amazing. And you might miss the chance to encourage a person who could do amazing things for Christ!

Whatever you do or say, do it as a representative of the Lord Jesus, giving thanks through Him to God the Father.

* COLOSSIANS 3:17

To be a representative is a great responsibility. A representative is the "face" of the organization she is representing. She gives people an immediate impression of that organization. She speaks to the public for the company she represents. She answers questions about it. She encourages others to become a supporter of what she represents.

YOU are a representative. That's what you do every day for God. The things you say and the things you do give others an impression of who God is.

ChallengePoint

Jesus was God's representative by speaking and acting with love for God and love for others. As God's representative now, is your love for God and others always the first thing people will see?

Knowing God by
Being Like Christ

In your lives you must think and act like Christ Jesus. Christ Himself was like God in everything. But He did not think that being equal with God was something to be used for His own benefit. But He gave up His place with God and made Himself nothing. He was born as a man and became like a servant.

✳ PHILIPPIANS 2:5-7

This verse is about a sin called entitlement. When you think you deserve things, you think you are entitled to them.

If there was ever anyone who had reason to think He deserved good treatment it was Jesus. After all, He was a human, but He was also God. As you read about His life on earth, you'll never read about Him being prideful or arrogant. He was treated very badly, but He treated others with respect. He didn't demand things from them. He even served others by washing their feet. Pride had no place in His heart.

ChallengePoint

Do you care more about yourself or others? Who is first in your heart? If it's others, you will be willing to serve them. That means doing things that you'd rather not do sometimes. It isn't always easy, but it is the way Jesus lived. Humbleness and a servant attitude are the models He gave you.

Knowing God by
Being Like Christ

Let us think of ways to motivate one another to acts of love and good works.

＊ HEBREWS 10:24

How would you like to have your own private cheerleader? She would walk around with you and do little celebration cheers when you do something good or something great happens for you. She would do encouraging "You can do it" cheers when you face something tough.

Weird, huh? But in reality you do have a cheerleader – Jesus is all about bringing out the best in people. When He was on earth He encouraged people to know God better which meant that they would treat others with love and look for ways to serve others. Do you give that kind of encouragement to others too? It means that you have to stop thinking only of yourself. You get to be someone else's cheerleader!

ChallengePoint

There are people cheering you on and you get to cheer others on. Are you willing to be a background person who encourages someone else to be the "star" once in a while? It's not easy. But being like Christ means that you don't think only of yourself. You look for ways to encourage and motivate others to be the kind of people God wants them to be.

Knowing God by
Loving Others

"The greatest way to show love for friends is to die for them."

✳ JOHN 15:13

Does this Scripture verse mean you have to die for your friends? Yeah, kind of, but not necessarily. You can show this kind of love for others by putting yourself and your wants in the background and focusing on someone else and how to help her succeed.

Jesus did lay down His life by dying, but He also laid it down by giving. He willingly served others by leaving heaven and coming to earth. So He gave up His own plans, agenda and desires. He gave up everything to come to earth because He loves us.

ChallengePoint

You can lay down your life for others by focusing on what's best for them. Put others first. When necessary, give up your ideas of how to spend your time and energy. Serve others by helping and encouraging them. Share God's love with others by giving, giving and giving some more. Time, energy, encouragement, money ... whatever they need.

Knowing God by
Loving Others

This is how God showed His love to us: He sent His one and only Son into the world so that we could have life through Him. This is what real love is: It is not our love for God; it is God's love for us. He sent His Son to die in our place to take away our sins.

* 1 JOHN 4:9-10

Has someone you love died? If so, you know that terrible sense of loss. You know how much it hurts and how very much you miss your loved one. Would you have willingly offered to give up the one you loved? Especially if you knew that loved one was going to be tortured before he died? Of course not. That's a ridiculous thought.

Here's a serious thought: God did that. He gave Someone He loved very much to people who ignored and killed the Gift, Jesus. God gave His Son willingly, knowing that Jesus would be killed by the very people He was given to. Why would He give so generously? Simple, love. God loves people. God loves you.

ChallengePoint

God couldn't have given a more precious gift of love to you. God's love is a gift to you. All you need to do is receive it. Thank Him for it. His gift of Jesus is just one evidence of His love. Every day in a multitude of ways He says that He loves you. Listen ... and tell Him you love Him too.

Knowing God by
Showing Courage

Be strong and courageous! Do not be afraid or discouraged. For the LORD your God is with you wherever you go.

＊ JOSHUA 1:9

Don't be afraid … right. Everyone is scared sometimes. Different things scare different people. But if someone says they are never afraid, they're lying. The comforting thing about this Scripture verse is the assurance, the promise, that you are never, ever alone.

You do not have to face the things that scare you alone. God is with you all the time. That means His power is going before you and also protecting you from behind. He's got you covered. So, you can face scary things with a little more courage. Call on God's strength to help you and remember that you are not alone!

ChallengePoint

If God is with you and all around you, what is there to be afraid of? OK, let's be realistic. You will be afraid sometimes and you know what – that's OK. But when you feel the fear start rolling around inside you, remind yourself that God is with you. Focus on that thought and let it push away the fear. It may take a while, and that's OK. Keep praying and reminding yourself that God is with you.

Witnessing His Power

He gives strength to those who are tired and more power to those who are weak.

✳ Isaiah 40:29

You know all about God's amazing power. The Bible is filled with stories about the miracles He did and the people He helped. That's great, but you probably want to know what that means to you. How do you experience God's power? Like this:

When you have a problem, ask God to help you. Look up verses about His power and strength. Memorize one that you really like. Say it over and over – especially when you're afraid or just worn out from fear. Notice the little things that happen; an encouraging word from a friend; something that is usually difficult gets easier. See the small ways God helps you. Eventually you will see that God's strength and power is growing in you!

ChallengePoint

God wants to strengthen you. He wants to help you. Try this system to see if you can experience more of God's strength and power in your life.

Knowing God by
Giving

If we have all we need and see one of our own people in need, we must have pity on that person, or else we cannot say we love God.

✱ 1 JOHN 3:17

Do you ever babysit young children? If you've been around a two-year-old, you've probably heard the word that age group seems to know best: MINE! Yeah, sharing is not a strong point for two-year-olds. God did not place you on this earth so that you could live like a two-year-old. You are not supposed to get as much stuff as possible, wrap your arms around it and shout, "MINE!" God's children share what they have with others … it shows that God's love is important to them.

There are people around the world who do not have enough … of anything. They don't have to wonder what to choose for dinner at night – they wonder if they will have any dinner. They don't have to choose what to wear each day – the clothes on their backs are all they have.

ChallengePoint

It's basically impossible to really, truly love God but ignore the needs of people around the world who are suffering because of war, drought, floods or earthquakes They need help. Your help. How can you share what you have? It's the God-thing to do.

Knowing God by
Suppressing Our Pride

Always be humble and gentle. Be patient with each other, making allowance for each other's faults because of your love.

This simple little verse contains four of the most difficult ways of living with others:

1. Be humble – life isn't all about you. It's about God, then others, then you.
2. Be gentle – don't push other people around to get them to do what you want.
3. Be patient – things don't always have to go your way.
4. Make allowances for others' faults – everyone messes up sometimes – even you. Don't scream about others' faults and brush your own aside.

Why do all of this? Love. Yep. God's love flowing through you to others.

Challenge**P**oint

No one said these things would always be easy. But they are important. You read often about them in the Bible. Living these ways are how you show God's love to others. If you can be humble, gentle, patient and make allowances, it shows that you understand that life isn't all about you.

Knowing God by
Abiding in Him

"Remain in Me, and I will remain in you. A branch cannot produce fruit alone but must remain in the vine. I am the vine, and you are the branches. If any remain in Me and I remain in them, they produce much fruit. But without Me they can do nothing."

* JOHN 15:4-5

Connections are important in your life. You are connected to your family. There is security in that because you know they love you. You are connected to your friends. That's cool because you belong to a group. You must also be connected to God. This verse explains why. To grow spiritually; to have long-term (eternal) meaning in your life, you have to be connected to God.

Your spirit's "food and water" come from Him. A branch chopped off a tree will die. If you don't stay connected to Him, your soul will literally starve to death. You need to be fed from His Word, by His love, and with His Spirit in you.

ChallengePoint

The only way to grow in God and make your life count for Him is to stay connected to Him. Get your spiritual food from His Word. Let Him guide and direct you as you talk with Him. Do what He has planned for you. This is possible if you stay connected to Him.

Knowing God by
Trusting Him

Let us hold firmly to the hope that we have confessed, because we can trust God to do what He promised.

* HEBREWS 10:23

There is a saying that kids repeat when they make a solemn promise to someone: "Cross my heart and hope to die." That means their promise is absolute truth and will not be broken.

When you say you're going to do something, do people know that they can absolutely, without a doubt, count on you to do it? Can you be totally trusted to follow through? If so, that's great. Not all people can be trusted like that. Sure, they mean to keep promises, but things get in the way sometimes and it's hard.

God wants you to know that you can absolutely, without a doubt, every single time, count on Him. When God says He will do something – it's law!

ChallengePoint

Do you know what God's promises are? You can know them by reading the Bible. When you read one of God's promises, then count on it. You can completely depend on Him and lean on Him. He's more solid than a rock.

Knowing God by
Using His Gifts

Christ chose some of us to be apostles, prophets, missionaries, pastors, and teachers, so that His people would learn to serve and His body would grow strong.

* EPHESIANS 4:11-12

A hot summer's day. A beautiful white sand beach. Ocean waves lapping against the shore. Big beach towel. A big bottle of water. Good book. Favorite tunes on your MP3. What could be better?

Yeah, that's a nice vacation, but don't settle in for a long laying-on-the-beach career. Everyone in God's family has a job. None of the jobs are full-time beach time. You have special abilities and talents that God gave you in order to help His work to be done on this earth. Maybe you don't yet know what your special abilities are, but as you keep learning about God, He will show you.

ChallengePoint

You may sometimes feel like "I'm just a kid. I can't do anything for God." Well, that's not true. In the Bible you'll read of some kids doing amazing things. Ask God to show you how He wants to use you. Think about what kinds of things you enjoy doing and that people often say you're good at. Your gifts probably are in that area.

Knowing God by
His Love

The LORD your God is with you; the mighty One will save you. He will rejoice over you. You will rest in His love; He will sing and be joyful about you.

✳ ZEPHANIAH 3:17

If you've grown up going to church, you've heard all your life that God loves you. So, by now its "old news" that sounds like *blah, blah, blah*. STOP RIGHT NOW and think about this – the God of the universe, God who created everything there is, God who keeps the oceans from running over the shores, who makes the stars stay in the sky, who sends the earth around the sun each day … that God loves YOU.

He not only loves you, He lives right here with you … among His people. Read this verse again – you make Him happy; so happy that He sings songs about YOU.

ChallengePoint

Do you sing when you're happy? Yeah, the music just rolls out of you, doesn't it? How does it make you feel to read that you make God so happy that He sings about you? It should take away any thoughts of "Yeah, yeah, I've heard about God's love before!" Does it make you feel really special? It should. God loves you … YOU!

Knowing God by
Praying

Pray continually.

* 1 THESSALONIANS 5:17

You're a girl … a female. One of the characteristics that females seem to have over males is that they can multi-task. OK, some males can, too, but overall women seem to do it better. So, when God says to pray all the time, you can learn how to do that. You may already know that it is possible to do more than one thing at a time. While you're doing things like playing sports, watching TV, even hanging out with friends, there are always thoughts running through your mind.

If your desire is to be in constant prayer, then you can focus those background thoughts as prayers. So, say you're walking down the street and you see someone walking by. You can whisper a little prayer for that person in your thoughts.

ChallengePoint

Praying all the time means that your thoughts constantly go back to God and you're aware of people around you and pray for them. It doesn't have to be a long prayer, just a breath prayer of one sentence, but still a prayer.

Seeking His Protection

I waited patiently for the LORD. He turned to me and heard my cry.

* PSALM 40:1

Honesty time: When your mom or dad calls for you to come and do something for them, how often is your response, "Just a minute … " Then, how long does that "minute" last? OK, flip that around. If you ask someone to come and do something for you and they say, "In a minute," how patient are you in waiting through that very long minute?

You see, the interesting thing about this verse is the word "patiently." When you're in danger and waiting to be rescued it is only possible to wait patiently if you absolutely trust that someone will come to help you. That means when you cry out to God for help and do not immediately sense His action, you don't give up. You KNOW He will help. He promised to hear your prayer.

ChallengePoint

Don't be discouraged if you don't feel you have a patient kind of trust right now. Seeking God's protection grows when you see a small way He protects you. Then the next time you seek His protection your trust is a little stronger.

Knowing God by
Seeking His Protection

He heals the brokenhearted and binds up their wounds.

✳ PSALM 147:3

Do you take a vitamin every day? Vitamins are a good way to make sure your body gets all the nutrition it needs to grow strong. Vitamins are a kind of preventive – they help prevent your body from getting sick.

Have you ever wondered why God doesn't more often take the preventive approach in protecting you? God can do anything. He has power over the whole world and anything that happens in it. So, why doesn't He just stop problems before they happen? Sometimes He does, in fact, probably more often than you know. Because since they don't happen, you don't even know what you've been protected from. However, bad things do happen. It stinks, but it's true. So where is God? Right there with you; loving you, caring for you, bandaging the wounds of your heart.

ChallengePoint

Of course you would prefer that God just fix the bad things – stop them from happening. But He doesn't always do that. However, when you hurt, He hurts, because He loves you. So His protection of you is to protect your heart when it's hurting, because that's when it is most vulnerable to Satan.

Jesus called out to them, "Come, follow Me, and I will show you how to fish for people."

* MARK 1:17

Fishing? Gross. You have to pick up a worm – actually touch a worm – and put it on a hook – put a hook through a worm? Sick. Okay, relax. Jesus didn't mean you would pull actual human beings out of a lake with a fishing rod. What would you use for bait? Cookies? That's just silly. When He said this, He was talking to fishermen and Jesus often used examples that made sense to the people He was talking to.

The point of Jesus' comment is that He will show you how to use your gifts to influence people to want to know Him better.

ChallengePoint

Not every person is a great preacher. Not everyone is good at sharing their faith with people on the street. But every Christian has abilities that can be used in God's service. Every person has something important – something that is part of God's plan to help others come to know Christ.

Knowing God by
Serving Him

We don't have the right to claim that we have done anything on our own. God gives us what it takes to do all that we do.

✳ 2 CORINTHIANS 3:5

Muhammad Ali was a world champion boxer who used to proclaim, "I am the greatest!" Yeah, humility was not his strong point, at least when it came to his boxing skills. People who brag about themselves, their successes or their abilities are no fun to be around. The thing is, no one really has anything to brag about because no one can take credit for their abilities or successes.

Everything comes from God – everything. Sure you may work to develop and strengthen your abilities – things like athletic abilities or musical talent – but the basic talent and even the strength and drive to develop it comes from God. No person has any reason to brag about anything. Instead, give praise and thanks to God for what He has given you.

ChallengePoint

God made you who you are. Whatever talents you have were planted in you by Him. He made you able to do what you can do. He wants you to use your skills for Him. That may mean something as simple (and easy) as giving Him the credit for your successes instead of holding a "Hurray for me" party.

Knowing God by
Serving Him

*Be careful to live properly among your unbelieving neighbors.
Then even if they accuse you of doing wrong, they will see your
honorable behavior, and they will give honor to God.*

* 1 PETER 2:12

In every school you get the "in crowd". And then you
get the girls who wish they were in the "in crowd". They
watch the in-crowd girls. They copy what they see those
girls do. They're watching.

There are people watching you, too, especially if they
know you are a God-follower. You go to church. You say
a quick prayer before lunch. Maybe you even read your
Bible. So … you're good, right? Well, there's a little more
to serving God … no, a lot more. How do you treat the
people around you? Are you kind? Are you loving and
forgiving? What kind of language do you use? What do
you watch on television? The point is that how you live
your life every day means something, especially to people
who do not know Christ. They are watching you.

ChallengePoint

Is it scary to think that you are serving God by the everyday
things you do? People are watching you. Do they see God's
love in you? Do they see His honesty and kindness in you
when you mess up and have to apologize? They are watching.

Knowing God by
Serving Him

Do your work willingly, as though you were serving the Lord Himself, and not just your earthly master.

✳ COLOSSIANS 3:23

There are some things in life that you have to do. Everyone has to do them. No one really enjoys them but they have to be done. What kinds of things? They could range from math homework to cleaning the bathroom to tidying up your room. Everyone has something they don't enjoy. Your enthusiasm is not so great for those no-fun jobs. That may mean that you don't do your best work, but just do enough to get by. That isn't good enough.

Everything you do is actually service to God. So, do your best – no matter what the job is. It may seem that what you're doing is a behind-the-scenes, not important, job. But everything you do reflects on God, because you are His child.

ChallengePoint

Remember that other people are watching you. How you do your job reflects your opinion of how important God is. So, always do you best and remember that in the end, you're doing this job for God, not for people.

Knowing God by
Obeying Him

LORD, tell me Your ways. Show me how to live.

* PSALM 25:4

Are you a leader or a follower? Some girls are born leaders and others follow them willingly. Some girls are followers who go where the leaders tell them to go. That's OK, but you have to be careful who you follow. Choose a leader who takes you on a path that brings you closer to God; a path of obedience to Him.

The best leader – the safest leader – is God Himself. Other leaders, human leaders, can be helpful if they are also God-followers, but God Himself will show you how to live. Read His Word and obey the commands you learn from it.

ChallengePoint

The beginning of obeying God comes from knowing what He wants you to do. The best way to learn that is by reading His Word and listening for Him to speak into your heart. He also guides you through the advice and opinions of Christian people around you (human leaders). Listen for His guidance, and then be willing to follow it.

Knowing God by
Obeying Him

We can be sure that we know God if we obey His commands. Anyone who says, "I know God," but does not obey God's commands is a liar, and the truth is not in that person.

* 1 John 2:3-4

Big talk. That's what it is called when actions don't match words. Promises made are just a lot of hot air. Words are easy … you can say whatever you want about how important God is in your life. But if your actions don't match what you say, then your words are just *"blah, blah, blah!"*

Don't bother talking about knowing God if you are going to do things that are directly disobedient to Him. God says that makes you a liar. What kinds of things are those? Saying mean things about other people, judging who is worthy of your attention, greed, looking at inappropriate websites, selfishness … it's a long list.

ChallengePoint

You can fool other people by saying the right "Christian" words. But you can't fool God. He sees your heart. He sees what you do in secret. He sees your thoughts. He insists on obedience … complete obedience.

The payment for sin is death. But God gives us the free gift of life forever in Christ Jesus our Lord.

✳ ROMANS 6:23

Have you been paid for a job? Perhaps a neighbor paid you to play with her children while she worked in the yard or maybe your parents paid you to do a job around the house. It is rewarding to be paid for your work. Have you ever been paid for doing something wrong; for disobeying? Yeah, not a payment you want to experience again probably.

Does it surprise you that there is payment for sin? Should you expect payment for doing wrong things? Well, the payment isn't good – it's being forever apart from God – death means being in hell forever. But God's love makes forgiveness possible. He forgives your sin and changes the payment to life forever with Him!

ChallengePoint

God's forgiveness of your sin is motivated completely by His amazing love for you. He wants you to be in heaven with Him forever, so He takes away the payment of death and celebrates that you'll be with Him in heaven. Ask Him to forgive you ... and thank Him that He does.

Knowing God by
Seeking His Guidance

The LORD grants wisdom! From His mouth comes knowledge and understanding.

* PROVERBS 2:6

A big project is due at school. You have months to work on it but you leave it all to the last week. Then, you work and work, but you don't get it done. So, you go to your teacher and try the old, "I didn't know when it was due" line. Yeah, doesn't work. It was your responsibility to know the requirements.

Along the same line, don't try telling God that you had no idea of the right thing to do when you have to admit doing something wrong. The "guide book" of right and wrong is right in front of you – the Bible. And if you ever have a question about whether something is a good thing to do or not … ask Him. He's willing to guide you and His guidance will be filled with wisdom.

ChallengePoint

Some rights and wrongs are easy to know. Some are not. God's guidance may not be as simple as, "Do this. Don't do that." Then again, it might be. Ask for His guidance, get into His Word and as you read it, let your mind and heart be quiet. You may find that a particular phrase or verse seems to jump off the page at you as God uses it to guide you.

Knowing God by
Understanding Anger

Don't be angry or furious. Anger can lead to sin.

✳ PSALM 37:8

Nothing good ever comes from getting angry. It may make you feel better for just a minute, but the long-term result is a broken relationship that may or may not be fixable. It usually goes like this:

1. Your friend makes you super-mad by saying something mean or untrue about you.
2. You're so mad that you completely lose control. You start shouting things at her without really thinking about what you're saying. All kinds of ugly junk comes out of your mouth.
3. Your friend stomps away. That friendship is toast.

God warns you against anger. When you get that angry, relationships are seriously damaged.

ChallengePoint

Over and over again God's Word focuses on love. Anger and love can't occupy the same space in your heart. God's focus is on how you respond and treat others. He also doesn't want your relationships to be damaged beyond repair. One way to prevent that is to keep your anger under control.

Knowing God by
Being Faithful

Lord, the heavens praise You for Your miracles and for Your loyalty in the meeting of Your holy ones.

* Psalm 89:5

Thank goodness for detail-oriented people. Maybe you are one. Do you keep detailed lists of things to do? Are you good at seeing the big picture of a project and then breaking it down into details so nothing is overlooked?

An example would be planning a huge cook-out and inviting all your friends. Your dad grills hamburgers and hot dogs. You get chips and salads. Everything is great ... except you forgot to get plates. Yeah, details.

One definition of faithfulness is conscientiousness. That means paying attention to detail from a sense of responsibility or devotion. God surely shows faithfulness in His work with His children. He takes care of you. He loves you. He guides you. He planned a way of salvation for you. No wonder the angels sing praises to Him.

ChallengePoint

Aren't you glad that God is detail-oriented? He is faithful. That's the bottom line. So, you can always depend on Him to do those things He promised to do for you. He's faithful. Praise Him for that.

His Faithfulness

If we are unfaithful, He remains faithful, for He cannot deny who He is.

* 2 TIMOTHY 2:13

Moods are the worst and girls are experts at them. Sometimes you don't even know why you slip into a bad mood. Your friends are probably experiencing moods too. It's hard because one day everyone is happy and friendly and the next day they aren't.

One wonderful thing about God is that He is not moody. God has made some very strong promises to His children. To love, protect, and guide them. None of these are based on what mood He is in. What does He ask from you? To love Him. What happens if you don't act loving toward Him? Does He take back His promises? Nope. He can't because God is love. That's who He is and He simply cannot act any other way.

ChallengePoint

Dealing with people's moods is frustrating. Dealing with your own moods is frustrating too. One day you're kind and helpful, and the next day you're a pain in the neck. God isn't like that. You can trust Him completely because you know He will always be the loving God He promises to be.

Knowing God by
Seeking Salvation

If you confess with your mouth, "Jesus is Lord," and believe in your heart that God raised Him from the dead, you will be saved.

✳ ROMANS 10:9

Your words can be good or bad, hurtful or encouraging. Isn't it interesting that such extremes can come from one person? Salvation is a gift from God, but it must be acknowledged and announced with your words:

1. Confess with your mouth that Jesus is Lord. That means say it out loud … publicly.
2. Believe that God raised him from the dead. Believe it, don't just say it. Know for sure that it's true.
3. Salvation is yours. Jesus is now living in your heart, loving, guiding and teaching. Heaven is your future – forever with God!

ChallengePoint

Salvation is a gift. Confessing Jesus out loud shows that you mean it and are willing to announce His Lordship to the world! God made the plan, but you have to open your heart to Him. It's not hard, but you do have to make the effort.

Knowing God by
Being Thankful

Be thankful in all circumstances, for this is God's will for you who belong to Christ Jesus.

＊ 1 Thessalonians 5:18

The "in all circumstances" is the hard part of this verse. It's easy to be thankful when you get good grades on tests, your team wins the championship, a sick loved one gets well, your mom or dad gets a great job, you're chosen for an honor … yep, when good things happen it's pretty easy to be thankful (if you remember to say thanks).

The "in all circumstances" is when things happen that aren't exactly what you would have chosen for your life. It is harder to be thankful then, right? Yeah, that's harder. Remembering that God is in control "in all circumstances" is the key.

ChallengePoint

Yes, God is in control of everything. Yes, He has a plan for your life. If you believe those two things, then thankfulness should come more easily. OK, sometimes it's hard to be immediately thankful when painful things happen, but if you believe those two statements, you will eventually be able to get to the thankful place.

The future is as bright as the promises of God.

~ Adoniram Judson

July

Knowing God by
Celebrating Him

The LORD your God has blessed everything you have done; He has protected you while you traveled through this great desert. The LORD your God has been with you for the past forty years, and you have had everything you needed.

* DEUTERONOMY 2:7

Everyone loves a party! Parties are fun because people are happy. There's lots of laughter and fun. Games and food! Any reason for a party works, right? Here's a good one – Celebrate God!

What does that mean? Here's a few ideas: Celebrate because you can read this book. Celebrate because you have a home. Celebrate because you have a family who loves you. Celebrate because you can attend church, read the Bible, pray to Him. Celebrate because you can go to school. These are a few reasons. Can you come up with more? God takes care of your every need (not "wants" but "needs"). Celebrate Him for all He does for you.

ChallengePoint

Wouldn't it be fun to actually throw a "Thank You, God" party? Encourage everyone who attends to make a poster of just one thing they are thankful for. God does so much for you every day – thank Him with a grand, happy heart celebration!

Knowing God by
Enduring

God is the one who began this good work in you, and I am certain that He won't stop before it is complete on the day that Christ Jesus returns.

✳ PHILIPPIANS 1:6

When you work on an art project it is a process. As you start the project it may not look too great. But you stick with it, keep working away, and slowly the beauty of the project emerges. It takes endurance to finish the job. Endurance is something you need to do – hanging in there when life gets tough.

Did you know that God also has the characteristic of endurance? It's true. He started doing good stuff in your heart – before you were even born and before you accepted Jesus as your Savior. He will keep doing that good work all the way until Jesus comes again and you're in heaven with Him. He will continue teaching you and growing your faith so that you are more like Christ.

ChallengePoint

So what this verse is saying is that you are always "under construction." God is continually working on you. That's kind of cool when you think about it. He never stops working to help you be better – more mature in your faith and more like the person He wants you to be.

Knowing God by
Being Like Christ

"I was hungry, and you gave Me food. I was thirsty, and you gave Me something to drink. I was alone and away from home, and you invited Me into your house. I was without clothes, and you gave Me something to wear. I was sick, and you cared for Me."

✳ MATTHEW 25:35-36

Some pictures on the evening news or even from missionary reports may tug at your heart. Seeing children who do not have enough food and only one set of old clothes may make you feel that "someone should do something." Guess what – you are that "someone." Jesus encourages you in these verses to think about others. That's a basic characteristic of being like Christ.

Jesus modeled caring for others first, without even thinking about how tired He was or what another day of healing people or teaching people meant to His tired body. He didn't worry about where His next meal was coming from or where He would sleep at night. He cared for others first and foremost.

ChallengePoint

These two verses show that being like Christ means caring for other people by actually doing something for them. By doing that you show your care for Christ Himself. Ask God to open your eyes to the needs of people around you.

Knowing God by
Being Like Christ

For we are God's masterpiece. He has created us anew in Christ Jesus, so we can do the good things He planned for us long ago.

✻ EPHESIANS 2:10

At times you may feel like a perpetual "B-teamer." If so, you feel like you haven't got much to offer; like there is always someone who can do things better than you. Well, here's a newsflash for you – you are God's masterpiece!

A masterpiece is an artist's finest creation; his best work. That's you – regardless of how you feel! He made you in His own image. That means you look like Him and act like Him. You can do many of the things God does – love, forgive, help, encourage.

And when you ask Jesus into your heart, you have even more of His fingerprints on you. Then it's even more obvious that you are like Him.

ChallengePoint

The cool thing about this is that the pressure is off you to achieve anything. God made you. He gave you gifts and talents. He wants to use you. You are God's masterpiece and you look like one of His creations. He has given you what you need to be more and more like Christ.

Knowing God by
Being Like Christ

Solid food is for those who are grown up. They are mature enough to know the difference between good and evil.

* HEBREWS 5:14

If you've done any babysitting you've probably given a bottle of formula to a baby. It's kind of funny smelling stuff, but babies seem to love it. When you're hungry though, you'd rather have a sandwich and maybe some sliced fruit or something to go with it. Since you started getting teeth, you don't really drink much baby formula anymore, you've grown beyond that.

Becoming more and more like Christ as you grow in your Christian life is like growing beyond baby formula. As you learn more about Him and become more like Him in the way you think and act, you can handle more mature Christian lessons and more responsibility.

ChallengePoint

Of course, growing more mature means more is expected. A baby doesn't know right from wrong, a ten-year-old does. Are you still drinking baby formula in your Christian life? Or are you learning more and more about Christ and becoming more like Him in how you live? If so, you are learning the difference between right and wrong – and choosing to live God's way more and more often.

Knowing God by
Loving Others

"But I am giving you a new command. You must love each other, just as I have loved you."

* JOHN 13:34

Loving your friends is super easy, right? You care about them and they care about you. So, what's the big deal about this "new command?" Well, Jesus didn't say, "You must love your friends." Nope, He said love each other, and that may mean loving people who you don't actually like. What? Is it possible to love someone you don't like? Actually, yes it is.

Love means putting other people's needs before your own. It's caring about what happens to them and how they feel and what they are going through. Loving others the way God loves you is … complete. Put yourself in the background and care for others.

ChallengePoint

Is this easy to do for people you don't really like? Nope. Is it necessary? Yep. Yikes. But thankfully, you don't have to do it alone. You can ask God to love others through you – especially people who are kind of hard to love. He will do it … and it takes a while, but pretty soon you'll start to notice a change in how you feel about those difficult people.

Knowing God by
Being Loving

Love never gives up, never loses faith, is always hopeful, and endures through every circumstance.

* 1 Corinthians 13:7

What does this Scripture verse teach you about God's love? Think about human love first … when someone hurts you over and over, eventually your love will lose hope that it's ever going to get better.

Human love is like a flame that can actually be put out. But God loves you no matter what. You may break His commandments – on purpose – having thought about it ahead of time and choosing to do so. He sticks with you time and time again. That's God's love.

Can you love Him back? No matter what? Do you trust Him completely, even when it feels as though He's not hearing your prayers and not doing what you think He should be doing? Do you love Him enough to trust Him, no matter what happens?

ChallengePoint

God's love is an incredible model of true love. It is steady, strong, and hopeful. Because of that He always hopes you will become more obedient and grow to be more like Christ. Does your love for Him reflect that same kind of strength and persistence? Can you love Him no matter what?

Knowing God by
Showing Love

And so we know the love that God has for us, and we trust that love. God is love. Those who live in love live in God, and God lives in them.

* 1 JOHN 4:16

Some clubs have membership requirements. For example, a French club may require that you choose a French name and that only French is spoken at meetings. All the members of that club are identified by their love of all things French. They probably have club jackets or sweaters that identify them to others too.

If you're a member of God's family, you will have identifying characteristics too. God is known by love. His character – the thing that defines God – is love. His love is seen throughout the Bible in the way He takes care of His people. You can see it in your life in the way He cares for you and guides you.

ChallengePoint

God is love. That's it. That's the bottom line. Everything about Him shows that love. You are His child, a member of His family and you should look like Him. Is His love evident in you?

Knowing God by
Showing Courage

Wait for the Lord; be strong and take heart and wait for the Lord.

* PSALM 27:14

The medical community suggests that at certain ages you be inoculated against various diseases. Getting a "shot" isn't much fun. In fact, some people have a real fear of needles. So, when you go to the doctor for an inoculation, if you have to sit and wait for your turn, you can get pretty nervous. Waiting makes it worse and pretty soon you're actually crying from fear.

When you're scared you have a tendency to get more and more anxious and build the situation into something much worse than it actually is. When you ask God to help you with something and you're waiting on Him, don't do that. God says to be brave enough to wait for Him to take care of things. You can trust Him because He loves you. So, wait patiently and with courage for Him to act.

ChallengePoint

Waiting is never easy. It's especially hard when you are afraid. But that is also the best time to learn that your faith in God can be trusted. He loves you. He will take care of you. So be brave and be patient. Trust Him to take care of you.

Knowing God by
Showing Courage

Finally, be strong in the Lord and in His great power.

✶ EPHESIANS 6:10

You don't need to be courageous if nothing scary is going on. You can just kind of glide through life. But when your parents split up, someone you love gets sick, a tornado rips through your town, can you depend on God? You can if you remember that His power and strength is fighting for you.

Don't let anything pull you away from Him. You can trust Him because His power is mightier than anything else in this world. What do you consider to be the most powerful thing in this world? Think about that for a minute. OK, now understand that God is more powerful than that. Way more powerful. So whatever you are facing, whatever is making you afraid, remember that you can trust God.

ChallengePoint

If you say that you trust God, then show it. When something happens that scares you, trust God to help you, protect you and love you. His power is stronger than anything life can throw at you and He loves you very much.

Knowing God by
Witnessing His Power

You made all the delicate, inner parts of my body and knit me together in my mother's womb. Thank You for making me so wonderfully complex! Your workmanship is marvelous – how well I know it. You watched me as I was being formed in utter seclusion, as I was woven together in the dark of the womb.

✳ PSALM 139:13-15

Ohhh, a baby. Don't you just love tiny little babies? They are so cute. Isn't it amazing that a newborn baby's body has everything she needs to become an adult. Think about that: the muscles she will need as a full-grown woman are there. The tiny, flexible bones in her feet will grow to be full-sized some day. Her brain will develop from not even knowing how to tell her body to roll over to being able to solve difficult math problems.

Amazingly all this stuff was put into this baby before she was even born. God creates every baby while she is being formed inside her mother. Each birth is a miracle of God's power and creativity!

ChallengePoint

Something as small and gentle as a newborn baby doesn't seem so powerful, until you really stop and think about it. Look around you – the people you see each day began life as babies, knit together by God. What a powerful miracle!

Knowing God by
Having Faith

God treats us much better than we deserve, and because of Christ Jesus, He freely accepts us and sets us free from our sins.

* ROMANS 3:24

When you talk back to your mom, are you punished? Sure, and you probably get what you deserve. (Mom's are not crazy about back talk, are they?) You can usually be thankful that you don't get what you deserve because it would usually be punishment, not praise.

God is the master of not giving you what you deserve. You have done nothing to deserve the amazing, giving love of God. You don't deserve to be forgiven of your sins. But God gives it because He loves you.

ChallengePoint

You can have faith in God's good gifts to you because He does love you so much. He will keep giving you what you do not deserve. Living by faith means learning to trust God in situation after situation. As you see Him work in one small way, your faith grows a little so you trust Him more the next time. Don't be discouraged if your faith wavers once in a while. It's a process to learn to trust Him. But it begins with the step of faith in trusting God for salvation – a fantastic, amazing, loving plan He made that you do not deserve at all ... it's given by love.

Knowing God by
Giving

On the first day of every week, each one of you should put aside money as you have been blessed. Save it up so you will not have to collect money after I come.

✳ 1 CORINTHIANS 16:2

Do you get an allowance from your parents? What has to come out of that money? Do you pay for your own lunch each day? CDs? Magazines? Movies? Snacks? Getting an allowance helps you learn to budget your money. Things cost money.

It also costs money to do ministry. Those people who have been called into a career of serving God need to be supported; supplies for doing ministry such as books and study guides cost money; running a church costs money. Those things are paid for by normal, everyday people giving some of their own money. This is God's instruction – to give money each day in some way to God's work.

ChallengePoint

The cool thing about this instruction is this: People who have a normal everyday job in their own town can have a part in reaching people for Christ around the world just by giving and supporting missionaries and church workers in other parts of the world. Cool, huh? Your offering can make a difference in someone's life on the other side of the planet!

Knowing God by
Abiding in Him

I sleep and wake up refreshed because You, LORD, protect me.

* PSALM 3:5

When you have a sleepover with your friends you all stay up late, giggling and talking and chowing down on snacks. It's fun, but are you rested and refreshed the next day? No way! You need a long nap to rest your body.

Rest is important to the body. On a typical night (no sleepover) you can sleep peacefully because you know God is on the lookout, taking care of you.

No matter what comes up you know He can take care of it, so you can sleep peacefully and not be worried about anything.

ChallengePoint

Peace that comes from abiding doesn't happen automatically, so don't get discouraged. Like most of life, it's a learning process to trust God enough to not worry about things. Don't get discouraged if you find you are still worrying once in a while, remind yourself that God is watching over you and that you can trust Him. Peace will come as you trust Him more.

Depend on the LORD in whatever you do, and your plans will succeed.

✴ PROVERBS 16:3

What's your dream for the future? Do you dream of being a professional singer? A nurse? A writer? A teacher? Apparently all you have to do to make your dream come true is depend on God and you become successful. Yeah sorry, that's not really what this verse means.

The most important part of the verse is the first phrase. It's important. Commit your actions to God. Depend on Him. Don't run into life doing your own thing. Pray and seek His guidance. Know that you're doing what He wants you to do. Then, you can trust Him to bless your actions because you are doing what He wants you to do.

ChallengePoint

God is not a big Santa Claus in the sky who will give you whatever you want. He wants to bless your work and your efforts, but make sure you are doing what He wants you to do. Commit your actions to Him. Pray for His guidance. Then thank Him for His blessings.

Knowing God by
Using His Gifts

Whatever is good and perfect comes down to us from God our Father, who created all the lights in the heavens. He never changes or casts a shifting shadow.

* JAMES 1:17

What's the best thing in your life? Your family? Your friends? Your home? Your pet? Your hobby? What's the thing that you look forward to most? Who is the person you most love to chat with?

Guess what? That person or thing – whatever it is – is a gift from God. He is the giver of all good gifts. It's good to remember that everything in your life is a gift from God. So, when you enjoy your favorite activity or when you look forward to hanging out with your favorite person … thank God.

ChallengePoint

Ultimately everything comes from God. He loves you so much that He gives and gives. He can't get enough of giving to you. Thank Him for His gifts and use them to the best of your ability.

Knowing God by
His Love

For you are a people holy to the LORD your God. The LORD your God has chosen you out of all the peoples on the face of the earth to be His people, His treasured possession.

✳ DEUTERONOMY 7:6

When teams are chosen in gym class, are you chosen first? Is your athletic ability so well known that any team captain wants you on her team? Being chosen first is very cool. It makes you feel special, set apart as better than average.

Did you know that you are chosen first and set apart as special to God? You are – you're a holy person to God, and holy means set apart. You know you're special because you are His treasured possession! He chose you. He didn't have to. He didn't need to have a special treasure – He's got all of creation. But He loves you so much that He considers you His treasure.

ChallengePoint

How cool is it to be chosen by God? Chosen ... the one He really wanted on His team! He thinks you are special. In fact, He treasures you. That's real love!

Knowing God by
His Love

The Father has loved us so much that we are called children of God. And we really are His children. The reason the people in the world do not know us is that they have not known him.

* 1 JOHN 3:1

You get to choose your friends and you usually do that because of what you have in common. You and your friends share interests and likes and dislikes. But you don't get to choose your family. They don't get to choose you either if you're born into a family. But you have a lot in common with your family. You have similar looks, characteristics and you share memories. Families are a very special place where you can be yourself and you know you belong.

The awesome thing about God is that He "adopts" you into His family when you ask Jesus to be your Savior. He calls you His child and He loves you as His child.

ChallengePoint

A father's love is deep and strong. It's a giving love that protects and guards. It's a love that wants to give as much as possible to his child. A father's love wants to teach and direct and help his child to grow into a mature young woman. God's love for you is a Father's love. Awesome.

Knowing God by
Praying

Don't worry about anything, but pray about everything. With thankful hearts offer up your prayers and requests to God. Then, because you belong to Christ Jesus, God will bless you with peace that no one can completely understand. And this peace will control the way you think and feel.

* PHILIPPIANS 4:6-7

Do you think that worrying is your spiritual gift because you are really good at it? Worry comes so easily, doesn't it? Worry seems easier than praying sometimes. Why is that? You wouldn't worry if you knew that all you had to do was mention your worry and it would go away. But God doesn't always act as quickly as you'd like Him to, does He? He doesn't do what you "tell" Him to do either. God doesn't always work on your time schedule or do what you think He should do.

That's where faith comes in. Tell Him what you are worried about. Trust Him to take care of it.

ChallengePoint

Giving up worrying for trusting and waiting is sometimes hard, right? After all, you've got the worry thing down pretty good. Take it a step at a time and learn to wait in faith. It comes with practice. When it does, God's peace will rule your heart.

Knowing God by
Seeking His Protection

For He will order His angels to protect you wherever you go.

* PSALM 91:11

Have you noticed the Secret Service men and women that go before, beside and around the president of the United States? Government leaders from all countries have them. These highly trained men and women have the singular job of protecting the person they are guarding. They keep the general public away from their person and scan the crowds, watching for anyone who might be up to no good.

Do you think it would be cool to have a Secret Service guard? Well, you do … kind of. God orders His angels to watch out for you and protect you wherever you go. You have a whole battalion of Secret Service watching out for you!

ChallengePoint

You have no idea how often God protects you when you don't even know about it. An angel may move over you to protect you from danger, or grab your shoulder to keep you from falling … you just don't know. But God knows. How cool is it to have His guards taking care of you!

Knowing God by
Seeking His Protection

Give all your worries to Him, because He cares about you.

* 1 PETER 5:7

This is the most awesome verse; especially for a worry-wart (that's a weird word, isn't it?) Everyone worries about something, but some are better at it than others. What do you do about worry? Just what this verse says: Tell God everything that worries you. *Everything* – from the biggies of parents splitting up to the everyday things of passing a test at school.

Beyond telling God – give Him the worry. Ask Him to take care of it by calming you down and helping you trust Him with the outcome of the problem. Ask Him to help you trust Him. You're going to need help with that so you don't grab the problem back and worry over it. He will take care of the problem and of you because He loves you.

The end.

ChallengePoint

Bad things are going to happen in your life. There's no way around that. How you handle them is up to you. Turn to God or worry yourself sick? Doesn't seem like a difficult choice, does it?

Knowing God by
Serving Him

Everything you were taught can be put into a few words: Respect and obey God! This is what life is all about.

* ECCLESIASTES 12:13

Serving God begins with two simple steps and they are outlined in this verse:

1. Respect God. This doesn't mean be scared of Him. It means honor Him with the respect that He deserves. Pay attention to Him. Don't "diss" God.
2. Obey His commands. First, you have to know the commands. They're in the Bible, so reading the Bible is implied here. Then, make the choice each day, several times a day, to obey them.

ChallengePoint

These two things are the first steps on the journey to serving God. If you don't respect and obey Him, serving Him is impossible. You must respect Him and obey Him, otherwise your relationship with Him is not worth much. Serve Him today, beginning with these two steps.

Knowing God by
Serving Him

Whoever wants to be a leader among you must be your servant.

✳ MATTHEW 20:26

Your friends who do not know God would never understand this verse. People who buy into the world's definition of success try to get as far from servant level as possible. They want to have servants, not be servants.

This verse turns the way the world looks at things upside down. A powerful leader would feel that her time should be saved for the "important things" while the servant does the boring or stinky jobs.

Jesus didn't agree. He said that a real leader is actually a servant. Jesus washed His disciples' feet. That was a servant's work. You should be like Jesus, and that means serving those around you.

ChallengePoint

Don't worry about being a leader. Don't worry about being a servant. Just look for ways to help others. Look for things to do for them that will let them know you care about them. Don't grumble about it. Don't brag about it. Just do it.

Knowing God by
Serving Him

So, do not let sin control your life here on earth so that you do what your sinful self wants to do.

* ROMANS 6:12

Whatever reigns in you rules you. It's in charge of what you do and how you choose to live. You have a choice every day. You can go with what the crowd does and do whatever they do, or you can put choices and actions through the filter of "What does God want me to do?"

You need to make an actual choice each day because if you don't actually make the choice to serve God you will be making the choice not to.

ChallengePoint

You serve God by obeying Him. That filter in your heart and mind that asks, "What does God want me to do?" is a good monitor for your choices. Don't let sin rule your life. Take a stand by choosing to serve and obey God.

Knowing God by
Obeying Him

God accepts only those who have faith in Jesus Christ. No one can please God by simply obeying the Law. So we put our faith in Christ Jesus, and God accepted us because of our faith.

✻ GALATIANS 2:16

Have you ever crammed for a test so that you knew the answers on test day but about an hour after the test you had forgotten pretty much everything? You missed the point of the test. It wasn't to dump out information; it was to actually learn something.

Obeying God is not the actual goal of the Christian life. Does that surprise you? The goal is to know Jesus and believe that Jesus, God's Son, came to earth, taught about God, was killed by His enemies, died willingly on the cross for your sins, was raised back to life, and now lives in heaven with God. Because of what He did, accepting Him as your Savior is what brings you into God's family. Not obeying laws for the sake of obeying.

ChallengePoint

Pharisees obeyed laws but they didn't believe Jesus was God's Son. They missed the whole point of their faith. God does not just want your obedience. He wants you to be part of His family. Knowing Christ as Savior is the only way for that to happen. Obedience to God's laws grows from knowing Christ.

Knowing God by
Obeying Him

The LORD has told you, human, what is good; He has told you what He wants from you: to do what is right to other people, love being kind to others, and live humbly, obeying your God.

* MICAH 6:8

Jigsaw puzzles have hundreds of pieces. Some of them have such complicated pictures that the pieces all look the same, so you can't look at a piece and figure out what part of the puzzle it might go with. It can take literally days to figure out the picture and put the puzzle together.

You don't have to worry about that kind of confusion when you are trying to obey God. He tells you right up front what is required. This verse gives you three simple parts of obeying: do justice or what is right (you know that by knowing the rules in the Bible); love kindness (be gentle and forgiving with others), and walk humbly with God (submit to Him and do what He wants).

ChallengePoint

Three simple steps. No, three steps. Not always simple. But these are a starting point to knowing how to begin a life of obeying God. It's a process to learn to obey more and more. But to begin, you must take the first step.

Knowing God by
Confessing Sin

At the name of Jesus every knee should bow, in heaven and on earth and under the earth, and every tongue confess that Jesus Christ is Lord, to the glory of God the Father.

✳ PHILIPPIANS 2:10-11

In some parts of our world today people are tortured and even killed for confessing faith in Jesus. That's terrible, isn't it? Why would they do that? Why wouldn't they just be quiet about their faith? Because when you really, truly believe in something, you are willing to take a stand for it even if it means torture or death.

Confession is important because it shows to the confessor, to the people listening, and to God Himself that the person speaking it believes it. God says that at some point in the future everyone will bow to Jesus. Everyone will know who He is.

ChallengePoint

If you knew you were going to be hurt for confessing your belief in God, would you do it anyway? God doesn't have much good to say about wishy-washy faith. If you believe in your heart, speak it with your mouth.

Knowing God by
His Forgiveness

Blessed are they whose transgressions are forgiven, whose sins are covered.

* ROMANS 4:7

Forgive and forget? Not easy to do. When someone hurts you it is hard to forget what she did. She may ask forgiveness and you may give it, but forgetting is a whole different thing. The hurt hides in the back of your heart and at some point in the future, if she hurts you again, that old hurt pops right back to the front and piles on to the new hurt.

God's forgiveness is not like any human forgiveness. When you ask God's forgiveness for your sin, He forgives and forgets – what you did is put out of sight. Forgotten. Over and done with.

ChallengePoint

God is so awesome. He forgives your sin and then forgets about it. He will never throw it back in your face again. It's over. You get to start fresh with a clean slate. God's amazing forgiveness is because of His love for you.

Knowing God by
Seeking His Guidance

You died to this life, and your real life is hidden with Christ in God.

※ COLOSSIANS 3:3

God has a plan for your life. He has had a plan for you since even before you were born. His plan for you is very connected to Christ. So, if you want to know what God's plans for your future involve, you need to get to know Christ better and better.

Does this verse mean that God's plan is really hidden; like a treasure? It means that Christ is the nucleus or heart of God's plan – everything revolves around Him.

Don't get the idea that God is trying to keep His plan a secret from you. No, but He does want you to get to know Christ better. That makes sense because His goal is for you to become more and more like Christ. Getting to know Him means you learn to be more like Him … which is God's plan for your life.

ChallengePoint

Sometimes people try to make learning about God a lot more complicated than necessary. God isn't trying to keep secrets from you. Why would He do that? He loves you. Christ is your model of how to live, so it makes sense that learning about Him answers the question of God's guidance in your life.

Knowing God by
His Faithfulness

Those who trust the LORD will find new strength. They will be strong like eagles soaring upward on wings; they will walk and run without getting tired.

✳ ISAIAH 40:31

Eagles are large birds. Yet, they spread their wings out and soar through the sky. Soaring isn't flying in the sense of flapping wings and working, it's sort of gliding through the sky. Soaring upward is harder than soaring downward.

God's faithfulness is so evident in this verse. Trust Him and nothing can bring you down in this life. Trust Him and His strength will help you fly high. It will help you soar. Trust Him and His strength will keep your strength coming. His strength will feed your strength. Trust Him and you will keep on keeping on. This is His promise to you and He always keeps His promises. He is faithful.

ChallengePoint

Does this mean you will never have problems? Of course not. Does it mean that trusting will always be easy? Of course not. Does it mean you will always fly high? Of course not. It means that God is faithful to be beside you, lifting you up when you fall, and strengthening you when you're weak. He is faithful to His promise to help you.

Knowing God by
Celebrating Him

Praise the LORD! Praise God in His sanctuary; praise Him in His mighty heaven!

* PSALM 150:1

Praise is celebration. Many of the psalms tell you to praise God. Why is it important to celebrate God? Because a typical person spends much of her prayer time asking God to do things. She asks Him to fix things, heal people, stop things, help with things. Those payers are a "to do" list for God. Of course, He wants to hear your prayers because He cares about the things that concern you. But once in a while, He wants you to stop asking and start celebrating.

Notice the things He has done for you in the past; the things He is doing right now and the promises He has given you for the future. Celebrate His power, His strength and His love!

ChallengePoint

Wow, it's so easy to get stuck in the "God, would You fix this thing?" mode. This verse is a reminder to try to balance your prayer time with celebrating God. Pay attention to all the wonderful things He does for you and gives you. Don't just say thanks, celebrate!

I may be little, but I'm BIG STUFF to God.

~ ANONYMOUS

August

Knowing God by
Enduring

I can do all things through Christ, because He gives me strength.
  * PHILIPPIANS 4:13

Do you have a dream? Your dream may be something so incredible that you won't even speak it out loud. You fear what kind of reactions others would have to your dream. Just for the sake of understanding, say that your dream is to be a prima ballerina. You know that to accomplish that you will have to work very hard. It will involve hours of classes and rehearsing. You will have to work so hard that your body will hurt, your feet may bleed … It would take real endurance to accomplish your dream.

Endurance means that you keep on going, working through problems, learning and growing. It means fighting through tiredness, injury or illness. It means you do not stop, ever, for any reason. Endurance is a great characteristic to have. In the Christian life that kind of drive comes from Christ's strength inside you.

ChallengePoint

Whatever your dream, Christ will be your strength to work toward it. When you live your life with Christ as your strength, the possibilities are endless. He will help you accomplish anything that He wants you to accomplish. So never give up and never stop trusting Him.

Knowing God by
Enduring

Control yourselves and be careful! The devil, your enemy, goes around like a roaring lion looking for someone to eat. Refuse to give in to him, by standing strong in your faith. You know that your Christian family all over the world is having the same kinds of suffering.

✳ 1 PETER 5:8-9

Your parents are probably continually trying to get you to pay attention to the world around you. Know that you can't trust everyone you meet. You need to pay attention. They are right … The devil is continually trying to trip you up. He doesn't want you to follow God. He's always on the look out for someone he can attack and some sneaky way he can trick you into turning away from God.

You must endure – stand firm against the devil. It's not easy because he is so sneaky and so persistent, but you can endure by being strong in your faith. God will help you by keeping you alert and He will help you to fight off the devil.

ChallengePoint

The devil is determined to pull you away from God. That's his goal. It is important to endure against him. Do not let him get even a tiny little victory in your life. Fight him by being strong in your faith. Stay close to God

August
3

Knowing God by
Being Like Christ

Our faces, then, are not covered. We all show the Lord's glory, and we are being changed to be like Him. This change in us brings ever greater glory, which comes from the Lord, who is the Spirit.

* 2 CORINTHIANS 3:18

You probably know that the moon doesn't really shine. It sure looks like it some nights though, doesn't it? It's a stark white light in the night sky. But it doesn't shine – it reflects light from the sun. The moon is a great reflector!

So are you. You reflect the Lord's light. But you can't reflect what you haven't seen. God, in His amazing grace, opens your eyes to see what Christ is like. Then, His Spirit helps you reflect Christ's image. You become more and more like Him as you see Him and reflect Him. The Holy Spirit is what makes the reflecting and changing possible.

ChallengePoint

Reflecting is your job, but ... you can't reflect what you haven't seen ... so ask God's Spirit to show you more and more of what Christ is like. Ask Him to help you understand what He shows you. The more you see Him and understand Him, the more likely you are to be changed into His likeness. Be a mirror that reflects Christ's image back to God. What a pleasing image that is!

Knowing God by Being Like Christ

Don't use foul or abusive language. Let everything you say be good and helpful, so that your words will be an encouragement to those who hear them.

✳ EPHESIANS 4:29

How often has your day been totally ruined by the words of a friend? It happens. She may say something that sounds really mean or accusing and whether she realizes it or not, her words lie like a brick on your heart.

Simple words can rip up a person's self-esteem. Christ didn't ever use foul or abusive language. Sure, He was firm sometimes, especially with the Pharisees, but when you read Christ's words, you see that while He was firm and honest, He always took the high road.

Christ taught that the second most important commandment is to love others. Language that hurts others doesn't go with that, does it?

ChallengePoint

What is abusive language? It is words that attack a person's character and intelligence; words that attack pretty much anything. That kind of language is never good or helpful and it is never an encouragement to others. Think about how the words you speak will land on another person's heart. Speak words that are positive and encouraging.

Knowing God by
Being Like Christ

God loves you and has chosen you as His own special people. So be gentle, kind, humble, meek, and patient.

✳ COLOSSIANS 3:12

Winning something is awesome – a beauty pageant, a spelling contest, any kind of contest. It's even good if you win because you are chosen, not because of something you did.

Read the verse above. Do you get it? God CHOSE you. He chose YOU to be His own! He chose you because He loves you. He loves you and wants to help you become more and more like Christ. He even gives you a list of characteristics right here that will make you more like Christ. Mercy, kindness, humility, gentleness and patience. Behaving in these ways will make you more like Him.

ChallengePoint

Being chosen is awesome. But after you're chosen you have some work to do, and these five characteristics are not easy to have every day. In fact, it's nearly impossible without God's help. But since He wants you to be like Christ and since He chose you to be His child, He will help you develop these characteristics.

Knowing God by
His Love

I love the LORD, for He heard my voice; He heard my cry for mercy.
* PSALM 116:1

When you settle down for a heart-to-heart talk with your friend you want all of her attention. It's frustrating to be spilling your guts to her while she's looking around to see who else she might want to talk with. You don't feel like she's really listening then, do you?

Part of the reason why you love someone is because she listens to you. She cares about you. Why do you love God? Can you list the things about Him that you appreciate the most? This verse shows one of the ways God loves you. He not only listens to you, He hears you. He cares about the things you care about and hears your cries for His help. That's one way you know God's love. He listens.

ChallengePoint

What other things about God's love do you most appreciate? Different things are special to different people. Think about a way God loves that means the most to you.

Knowing God by
Showing Love

Even more than all this, clothe yourself in love. Love is what holds you all together in perfect unity.

✴ COLOSSIANS 3:14

Honesty time: How much time do you spend each day deciding what you're going to wear and how you're going to do your hair? Come on, be honest. You get up in the morning and put on your clothes. You choose an outfit that makes you look good and that will make you feel more confident. So, it is agreed that you spend a certain amount of time on your outward appearance.

You have another choice of something to wear each day. It involves your inward appearance. It is love. God is love and His Word tells you how important it is for all of His family to be dressed in love as He is. Love pulls you together with others. It shows that you belong to God.

ChallengePoint

Love is what binds God's people together. It's the characteristic that shows you belong to God. Wear love every day and let it show in the way you speak to others and the way you treat others.

Knowing God by
Showing Courage

I am proud of the good news! It is God's powerful way of saving all people who have faith, whether they are Jews or Gentiles. The good news tells how God accepts everyone who has faith, but only those who have faith. It is just as the Scriptures say, "The people God accepts because of their faith will live."

* ROMANS 1:16-17

Shame is an awful emotion. It's no fun. You can feel shame because you take a stand for God and someone makes fun of you for it. Then you learn how strong your belief in God is. How courageous are you in taking a stand for Him? Are you willing to risk what people might think about you because you follow God?

It takes courage to let people know you are a Christian. It could mean that others make fun of you. It could mean that you choose not to do some things that other kids do. But remember that courage to share the story of God's love with others also gives others the chance to know Him.

ChallengePoint

Your courage to stand for God and to share His love with others is very important. It gives others the chance to learn about God. If others see that your faith in God means enough to you to be brave enough to share it, they just may listen.

Knowing God by
Witnessing His Power

"I am the Alpha and the Omega – the beginning and the end,"
says the Lord God. "I am the One who is, who always was, and
who is still to come – the Almighty One."

* Revelation 1:8

Alpha and Omega means first and last. While some girls are so puffed up with pride that they think they are the most important … they are wrong. After all, who was here in the beginning? God – He made everything there is. He created the world out of nothing. Who is here now? God – He walks beside you every day. He knows what will happen in your life before it even happens. He guides and protects you. Who will be here in the future? God – One day He will bring His children to heaven and get rid of Satan forever.

God's power is shown in His constant presence. No puffed-up-with-pride girl can match any of that.

ChallengePoint

So what should God's presence in the beginning, now, and in the future mean to you? It means He is more important than any bully girl who thinks she can tell you what to do and what to believe. When everything else is gone … when everything that seems to be so powerful is gone … God will still be here. He is the only thing that will endure to the end and beyond.

Giving

It doesn't matter how much you have. What matters is how much you are willing to give from what you have.

* 2 CORINTHIANS 8:12

A big part of giving to God's work is attitude. Do you understand that giving to God's work is a privilege? It's a way of worshiping Him. How? Giving to His work shows that you believe in it and that His offer of salvation to humanity is important to you.

The key is your attitude about giving. If you give grudgingly and wishing you didn't have to, then you aren't going to consider it a privilege or worship. If you give eagerly, glad to help and excited by the chance to be a part of His work, then you will be worshiping as you give. It doesn't really matter if you have one dollar to give or one hundred dollars. Your attitude is most important. Knowing you are a part of God's work because of your own generosity connects you with God's people!

ChallengePoint

It's interesting that attitude makes such a difference, isn't it? Being a part of God's work in your town or in another part of the world is a privilege. Give with the right attitude and enjoy the blessing.

Knowing God by
Suppressing Our Pride

He mocks proud mockers but gives grace to the humble.

⁎ PROVERBS 3:34

Pride never does good things for the people around it. When a girl is puffed up with her own importance she tends to make fun of others, pushing them down as she lifts herself up. It's not fun to be around a proud person. Girls who brag about themselves don't really convince anyone of how wonderful they are. The only people who think a braggart is awesome is the braggart herself.

Remember God's focus for you? It is to love others. Bragging about your own accomplishments, skills, brains, looks or anything else does not show love to others. When you push down your own pride and lift others up by complimenting their successes, you are living the way God encourages.

ChallengePoint

Some people brag about themselves because no one else will. But instead of doing that they should be noticing others' successes and talents. They should encourage them to use their skills and talents for God's work. Lift others up!

Knowing God by
Trusting Him

*Since we have a great High Priest who rules over God's house,
let us go right into the presence of God with sincere hearts fully
trusting Him. For our guilty consciences have been sprinkled
with Christ's blood to make us clean, and our bodies have been
washed with pure water.*

✳ HEBREWS 10:21-22

OK, you ask your mom if you can go to Jen's house.
But you don't really want to go to Jen's, you want to
go to Ashley's house because her parents aren't home.
But you know Mom will say no. So you pretend to go to
Jen's house but go to Ashley's. Cool plan … until you get
caught. When you get home, Mom sits you down and …

It's a scary feeling to get caught and have to face your
punishment. Do you feel that same kind of fear about
coming into God's presence? Don't you trust the fact that
God loves you? You know He does because He has made
you clean from your sin by the death of His own Son,
Jesus. That's love you can trust!

ChallengePoint

Knowing that you can trust God should take away a lot of
fear. Of course you still respect Him and honor Him, but trust
and fear don't live in the same place. If your heart is filled with
trust for God, then you have nothing to fear.

Knowing God by
Trusting Him

"Don't let your hearts be troubled. Trust in God, and trust in Me."

✳ JOHN 14:1

You climb into bed with an anxious feeling in your stomach. You toss and turn, glance at the clock and see it's 11:30 PM. You toss and turn some more. Glance at the clock again and see 1:30 PM. On and on through the night. You are majorly troubled. Anxiety, fretting, worry and fear are all characteristics of a heart that does not trust God.

What causes your anxiety? It could be anything from a big exam at school, giving an oral book review, problems at home, parents splitting up or major illness. Whatever it is it means you can't get the issue off your mind. You're constantly trying to figure out how to "fix it." When you realize you can't fix it, then you worry about it. As the worry grows you get scared. Wow, exhausting, huh? That whole process can be avoided by simply trusting God.

ChallengePoint

When things are going great you may declare how much you trust God. Yeah, but you don't really know if you trust Him until problems come. When things get tough, do you believe completely in His love and care for you? That He will take care of you and that He always has your best interests in mind?

Knowing God by
Using His Gifts

Because of God you are in Christ Jesus, who has become for us wisdom from God. In Christ we are put right with God, and have been made holy, and have been set free from sin.

* 1 CORINTHIANS 1:30

It seems like every week there is some new techno gadget on the market. The computer age started a landslide of inventions from wireless Internet to MP3 players, cell phones and who knows what else. It's really cool to have all these gadgets available though. It makes your life a lot easier than the olden days when letters were delivered by Pony Express.

Do you use all the modern conveniences available to you? Sure you do. It would be silly not to. It just makes sense to use everything available. They make your life easier, better and safer. In the same way, you should use all of God's gifts that are available to you. He makes available His own wisdom, strength, power, holiness – everything about Himself – through Jesus.

ChallengePoint

God makes so much available to you and all you have to do is accept it and use it. So simple. The Christian life and living for God is so much easier if you accept God's gifts. Thank Him for them. Use them. Grow with them.

Knowing God by
His Love

God shows His great love for us in this way: Christ died for us while we were still sinners.

* ROMANS 5:8

What was the best gift you ever gave to someone? What made it so good? Was it expensive or did you spend a lot of time making it? Would you have given such an awesome gift to someone who always treated you really bad? Yeah, maybe not.

But compare your act of generosity to God – He willingly gave His only Son to humanity, even while they were rejecting Him and disobeying Him. He showed His incredible love for you even before you decided you loved Him and would obey Him.

He loved you first, not knowing if you would choose to love Him back.

ChallengePoint

Since God loves you that much, what's your response to Him? His love is so deep, wide, strong and powerful that it's impossible to measure it. Does the generosity of His love for you cause you to want to love Him more?

Early the next morning, while it was still dark, Jesus woke and left the house. He went to a lonely place, where He prayed.

∗ MARK 1:35

Honesty time: How much time do you spend talking with your friends? What about your best friend? Your friend time is probably the focus of your week, and all the other stuff fits around it, right? Talking with your friends is important! OK, how about your talking time with God? Do you connect with God every day?

This verse shows that you need a daily connection to Him. You may be smart, wise and strong, but if Jesus needed to pray every morning, then so do you. This verse is just one example of how important prayer was to Jesus when He lived on earth. Even if He had spent a long day teaching and healing, surrounded by crowds of people, He still focused on connecting with God, even if it meant getting up before sunrise to have time to do that.

ChallengePoint

When you have an example to follow it is easier to figure out how to do something. Jesus is your example of how to live for God. For Him prayer – conversation with God – was very important. Start every day by connecting with God and asking for His guidance and help throughout the day.

Knowing God by
His Love

May you have the power to understand how wide, how long, how high, and how deep His love is. May you experience the love of Christ, though it is too great to understand fully. Then you will be made complete with all the fullness of life and power that comes from God. Now all glory to God who is able to accomplish infinitely more than we might ask or think.

      * EPHESIANS 3:18-20

Do you like to read mysteries? Do you enjoy trying to figure out the ending based on the clues the story gives you? There are some real-life mysteries that are just too big to figure out. You will never understand them in this life. The size of God's love is one of those things. It's so big that it's impossible to comprehend. Yet, God wants you to experience it more and more so that you understand it better and better. His love gives you power – His power – to live life to the fullest.

ChallengePoint

By experiencing God's love in your life you begin to understand it a bit. Spend some time each day thinking about what God has given you that day. Think about the ways He shows His love to you. Think about the things He helps you accomplish. As you think about Him you'll begin to understand His love a little more all the time.

Seeking His Protection

The LORD is good. He protects those who trust Him in times of trouble.

* NAHUM 1:7

Where do you go when you're scared? Who can you trust to protect you? Hopefully, your home is a safe place. You can trust your parents to protect you. But remember that the safest place to run is to God.

Some girls look for safety and protection from friends, in activities, in work, in success. What they don't realize is that those things will cave in when things get tough. God will not. He will protect you from anything and everything. All you have to do is come to Him and trust Him to take care of you.

ChallengePoint

There is no denying that the trusting might be the hard part here. Remember that God doesn't promise to keep you from trouble but He does promise to be with you when troubles come. Sometimes it's tempting to turn and run when problems get bigger instead of smaller. Fight that temptation. Stay close to God and let Him guide you through the hard times. Ask Him to make you stronger through your problems.

Knowing God by
Serving Him

"If you give even a cup of cold water to one of the least of My followers, you will surely be rewarded."

✳ MATTHEW 10:42

OK, say you are willing to serve God but you want your service to be something big and noticeable. Say you don't really want to serve by helping someone who is super poor and maybe even undesirable.

But serving God is often in the simplest of things. Serving God is just paying attention to people around you. Noticing what they need and thinking about how you can help them. Something as easy and simple as offering a drink of water to someone who is thirsty. Serving God requires a willingness to help whomever God brings across your path.

ChallengePoint

Serving God begins with paying attention to people around you. Don't get so caught up in your own life or problems that you only think about yourself. Serve God by looking around and seeing what simple thing you can do to show someone else that you care ... and that God cares.

Knowing God by
Serving Him

Dear friends, God is good. So I beg you to offer your bodies to Him as a living sacrifice, pure and pleasing. That's the most sensible way to serve God. Don't be like the people of this world, but let God change the way you think. Then you will know how to do everything that is good and pleasing to Him.

* ROMANS 12:1-2

In the 2008 Olympics a young swimmer named Michael Phelps amazed everyone by winning eight gold medals. Three medals were because of relay teams with three other swimmers. Michael and his relay teammates had all given their entire lives and bodies to getting ready for their races. They had each spent years practicing, eating high-calorie diets and getting plenty of rest. Each swimmer's focus was on preparing to win their races.

Each believer's effort to serve God should be just as intense. God doesn't ask for just an hour a week, He asks for your entire body and mind to be given to Him.

ChallengePoint

Being completely focused on serving God changes the way you think. It changes the way you live. After a while your heart is changed. You don't think the way they think or act the way they act. Your life is defined by service to God. What could be better?

Knowing God by
Obeying Him

"If you love Me, you will do what I have said, and My Father will love you. I will also love you and show you what I am like."

✳ JOHN 14:21

There is a simple way to know if someone really and truly loves God. If the person obeys God's laws then it is possible she loves God. If you obey His commands it will show in the way you live and the way you speak – if you don't obey them, that will show too.

So, you can spout words about loving God, but if you are unkind to others, selfish, jealous, gossipy … more than likely your words are just words. Obeying God is evidence of loving God. The more you obey Him, the more you will learn about Him. You get to learn more as you show Him that you are obeying what you do know.

ChallengePoint

You can't obey what you don't know, so read His Word to find out how you should be living. The first step to obeying God is knowing Him.

Knowing God by
Obeying Him

You have accepted Christ Jesus as your Lord. Now keep on following Him.

＊ COLOSSIANS 2:6

When you play a video game, you start at Level One and hope to improve your game skills so you can move up and up in the levels. Improving is always the goal.

God has high ambitions for you too. That's why He says that accepting Jesus isn't the end of the journey for you. If you continue to follow Him, you will learn so much more about living for Him. That's God's goal for you.

How do you begin the journey to follow Jesus?

1. Read God's Word. You'll learn God's commands for your life from it. You'll also see how Jesus lived on this earth. How He interacted with others and how He honored God. You can learn a lot from studying Jesus.
2. Pray. Talk to God and then be quiet and listen for Him to speak to your heart.

ChallengePoint

Two simple steps = big rewards. God's high goals for you begin here.

Knowing God by
Confessing Sin

Anyone whose name was not found recorded in the Book of Life was thrown into the lake of fire.

✳ REVELATION 20:15

Would you do something like jump out of a plane without a parachute? Play with fire? You wouldn't take stupid chances with your life. If you don't confess your sins to God, then you are taking some major chances with your future. God takes confession very seriously.

Confession, which is admitting your sins to God, shows that you are willing to be honest with God. Part of confessing is asking for God's forgiveness. If you don't trust God enough to confess, then you must question whether your relationship with Him is real. If it's not real then you will not be joining God in heaven. God is very firm about that. Remember, God takes confession seriously.

ChallengePoint

Don't you see that confession is an important part of your relationship with God? Make it part of your daily talk with Him. Confess wrong thoughts, actions and attitudes. Ask for forgiveness and ask for His help in correcting those things.

Knowing God by
His Forgiveness

"I promise you that any of the sinful things you say or do can be forgiven, no matter how terrible those things are. But if you speak against the Holy Spirit, you can never be forgiven. That sin will be held against you forever."

✳ MARK 3:28-29

Is there something that a friend might do which you would refuse to forgive? What if she told a major lie about you to a boy you liked? What if she told your parents that you had been lying to them about something? What is unforgivable? Is there anything you might do that God could never forgive?

Just in case you think you have been so bad that God could never forgive you – or would even want to – this verse sets that straight. Any sin can be forgiven, even being disrespectful to God. He really wants to forgive you. However, don't feel that His willingness gives you the freedom to do whatever you want. God does have a bottom line.

ChallengePoint

God's bottom line is when a person disrespects the Holy Spirit and His power and work in her life. Think before you speak about Him. Pay attention to your attitudes. Otherwise, confess your sins to God and believe that He will forgive you.

Knowing God by
Seeking His Guidance

When people's steps follow the LORD, God is pleased with their ways.

✳ PSALM 37:23

The members of a marching band spend a lot of time learning their routines. Each member's steps are ordered by the band director. If one band member doesn't follow the rules it messes up the entire routine.

Your steps are guided too – by God. But don't wait for God to guide you if you aren't submitting to Him. That means this: God wants to guide you and He will, but not if you haven't asked Jesus into your heart. After that, the next step is to seek God's guidance. Obey the knowledge you have; the commands you know. If you aren't doing that, don't seek more guidance in other areas of life.

ChallengePoint

Some of God's commands are very clear – the Ten Commandments for example. If you aren't making any attempts to obey the commands you have, then don't bother to ask for guidance in other things. Guidance comes in steps ... do your part.

Knowing God by
Being Like Christ

If you do the right thing, honesty will be your guide. But if you are crooked, you will be trapped by your own dishonesty.

* PROVERBS 11:3

It stinks, but sometimes good guys lose and bad guys win. It would be nice if God would change this pattern, but people who are dishonest seem to keep getting ahead. The more rotten things they do the more successful they are. It's frustrating!

Well, have faith, because these people will eventually get what's coming to them. Being like Christ means being guided by honesty and treating others in the way you would like to be treated. People who are consistently dishonest will one day answer for that – to God.

ChallengePoint

It may not help you right now, but someday those who have lived by dishonesty; cheating others and lying to them, will pay. Living that way is as un-Christlike as you can get. All people will one day stand before God to be judged, and that dishonesty will be answered for then, if not before. Live like Christ – guided by honesty.

Knowing God by
Being Like Christ

Christ will make His home in your hearts as you trust in Him.
Your roots will grow down into God's love and keep you strong.

✳ EPHESIANS 3:17

There was a little book written a long time ago called *My Heart, Christ's Home*. It's about Christ living in your heart. It's interesting because all the things hidden in the person's heart are then known to Christ. Some of that isn't good.

Are you hiding things in your heart that you would be embarrassed for Christ to know about? Are you making your heart a comfortable place for Him to be? Are your actions and thoughts things you want Him to know about? Better make sure your heart is clean since He's there all the time.

Actually, He will help you learn to be obedient. As you trust Him more and more, your understanding of God's love will grow deeper and you will be stronger.

ChallengePoint

Since He lives in your heart Christ is with you all the time. You probably like that when you have needs you want Him to take care of. But this verse is a good reminder during the times when you might be just as happy if He wasn't around. He is. Live your life in a way that pleases and honors God.

For our high priest is able to understand our weaknesses. He was tempted in every way that we are, but He did not sin.

* HEBREWS 4:15

This verse is an honest reminder that yes, God understands gossip, He understands selfishness. Because of this Scripture verse you can't say He doesn't understand the temptation to cheat, or the urge to tell a lie to protect yourself. He does understand.

This verse tells you that Christ experienced the same kinds of temptations to protect Himself and promote Himself as you do. Read about Satan tempting Him in Matthew 4. He understands. He's been through it.

ChallengePoint

Christ can help you with your problems because He knows and understands what you struggle with. He can help you because He experienced temptation Himself. He will help you stand strong – just as Christ did when He faced heavy temptation.

Knowing God by
Loving Him

Love the LORD your God with all your heart, all your soul, and all your strength.

✳ DEUTERONOMY 6:5

Give 100%. That's what this verse is saying. Don't give 50% of your energy to God and 50% to something else. God insists on 100%. Why? God loves you completely.

From the simple little chorus you learned as a child, "Jesus loves me this I know; for the Bible tells me so" to heavy-duty verses such as John 3:16, you know that God holds nothing back. He gives everything to you. His focus is you, all the time! He thinks about you, sings over you, celebrates with you. His Word says that He considers you His masterpiece.

He asks that you love Him back just as completely and intently.

ChallengePoint

Don't try to bluff your way through life with God. Love Him with all your heart, soul and strength. That means that nothing at all comes before Him – nothing. It means that He is the most important to you, not friends or popularity or music or a sport or hobby. It means that nothing comes between you and your desire to serve Him and know Him better. Nothing.

Loving Others

May the Lord make your love grow more and multiply for each other and for all people so that you will love others as we love you.

✳ 1 THESSALONIANS 3:12

The very fact that some people are hard to like, let alone love, is proof that you need God in your life in order to fully love others. It is important to God that you love others – not just your family and friends – but all people.

You know it's important because it is mentioned over and over in the Bible. Admittedly, some people are not easy to love. But look at the first phrase of this Scripture verse: "May the Lord make … " How cool is that! God will help you as you strive to love all people. It's important to Him, so He will help!

ChallengePoint

God knows that certain people are hard to love. He knows that as you look around the world, certain cultures may be hard for other cultures to love. But it matters to Him that people love each other more and more. So, He will help. How? He will slowly soften your heart toward people and help you notice some good characteristics about them. It may be slow, but He will do it.

Knowing God by
Showing Courage

Put on every piece of God's armor to resist the enemy in the time of evil. Then after the battle you will still be standing firm.

* EPHESIANS 6:13

It may not be a common thing to see a girl wearing armor. But don't get hung up on that. Instead, think about the lesson to be learned from this verse. What do you know about armor? Different pieces of armor protect different parts of the body. God provides exactly the armor you need to resist the devil's attacks. The devil knows where your weak areas are; gossip, pride, greed, for example. So, put on the piece of armor that protects that part of the body.

You can be courageous as you fight off Satan if you use what God has provided. God doesn't expect you to fight this sneaky enemy in your own strength. Your courage comes from knowing you aren't alone – and because you use the armor God provides.

ChallengePoint

Everything you need to fight Satan is provided by God. Read Ephesians 6 to learn about the parts of the armor that will help you win each battle. Put the armor on and courageously stand strong!

God carries you close to His heart.

~ Anonymous

September

Knowing God by
Suppressing Our Pride

"For whoever exalts himself will be humbled, and whoever humbles himself will be exalted."

✳ MATTHEW 23:12

Girls who are so impressed with themselves that they talk about themselves all the time are filled with pride. These kinds of girls need to have everyone notice them and think they are something special.

On the other side are girls who are so humble that they never say a word about themselves, but always find ways to encourage others into the spotlight.

Which person pleases God? Not hard to figure out, is it? The humble person pleases God.

ChallengePoint

God's focus is always, always on others. That's His focus for you too. Lift others up. Encourage others. Love others. If you're busy bragging about yourself you won't be helping anyone else. Please God by encouraging others, not by bragging about yourself.

Knowing God by
Abiding in Him

Those who go to God Most High for safety will be protected by the Almighty.

* PSALM 91:1

You and your friends pack a picnic lunch and head to the park. It's a hot day and the sun is beating down. So, at the park you look for a nice shady spot under a tree to have your picnic. Shade – a welcome thing on a hot summer day. Shade is pleasant because it blocks the rays of the hot sun beating down on you.

God is like shade for you too. When you stay close to Him, in the shelter of His presence, then you are protected from the heat of Satan's attacks. As long as you're in God's shadow you know you're safe.

ChallengePoint

Abiding in God is a daily decision. Satan tries every day to break up your relationship with God. He doesn't want you to abide in God. But being in God's shadow means you are close to Him, and that's the safest place to be.

Knowing God by
Trusting Him

Blessed are those who trust in the LORD and have made the LORD their hope and confidence.

✳ JEREMIAH 17:7

When a gymnast stands on the 4-inch wide balance beam, raises up on one foot and spins around, how does she keep from getting dizzy and falling off? How does she know when she is at the front and it's safe to put her foot down again? A gymnast might tell you that she focuses. She fixes her eyes on one spot before the spin begins and she watches for that same spot again to know when to stop.

Focus is important in the Christian life. Being blessed means being very happy and having good fortune. That's what you get from trusting God completely. Keep your focus directly on God and pleasing and obeying Him. That leads to trust, which leads to being blessed.

ChallengePoint

Trusting doesn't just happen automatically. Learning to trust is a process. You can probably trust God a bit right away, but by trusting Him a little you learn to trust Him more the next time a problem comes up. More trust leads to more confidence and a better understanding of how much God loves you.

"Only people who don't know God are always worrying about such things. Your Father in heaven knows that you need all of these. But more than anything else, put God's work first and do what He wants. Then the other things will be yours as well."

✳ MATTHEW 6:32-33

Parents are awesome, aren't they? Your mom and dad do their best to provide everything you need as a child. They make sure you have food, a home, a bed to sleep in, clothes to wear. You don't have to worry about anything. Wow, well read today's verses again and see how God takes care of you.

People who don't know God have to worry about how to get everything themselves. They have to be concerned about protection, power and success. As God's child, you don't really need to worry about that stuff. God knows what you need. He will take care of you. Your job is just to get to know Him and live in obedience to Him.

ChallengePoint

Knowing God does not guarantee that you will be rich or famous. Don't try to make this Scripture verse mean that. God will supply what you need (not want), but you must live obediently for Him. Seek Him.

His Love

As high as the sky is above the earth, so great is His love for those who respect Him.

✳ PSALM 103:11

It's so cool to be out, away from the city on a dark, clear night. When you look up at the sky you see a bazillion stars! It's so beautiful. It's amazing to think that the farthest star is millions of miles away from earth and the light from it that you're seeing actually left it years ago.

God's love for you is bigger than that distance. Look around at the hundreds of stars you can see in the sky. The night sky looks endless, doesn't it? God's love is bigger. It can't be measured. He loves you very, very much!

ChallengePoint

There are really no words to describe how big and wide God's love is. But what means the most is the personal love. He loves you. YOU.

The LORD is close to all who call on Him, yes, to all who call on Him in truth.

> * PSALM 145:18

Do you sit in the family room and scream at the top of your lungs when you want your mom's attention? "M-O-O-O-M!!!!!!" Does she answer? Wouldn't it make more sense to get up and go to the room where your mom is?

It's easier to talk to someone when you're close by them. Well, how about that? That means it's easier to talk to God when you're close to Him, right? Stay close to Him by reading His Word, speaking to Him and spending time quietly thinking about Him. When you do, He is right there to help you, guide you, give you wisdom and bless you.

ChallengePoint

Do you understand what an amazing privilege prayer is – the right to talk to God. He came up with this plan and hopes that you will take advantage of it in order to know Him better and to experience His closeness to you.

Knowing God by
Seeking His Protection

I pray that God will take care of all your needs with the wonderful blessings that come from Christ Jesus!

* Philippians 4:19

Don't get overly excited – this verse doesn't mean you're going to get every gadget or piece of designer clothing you have ever dreamed of. The key to this verse (and something you may not think about very often) is that it says "need" not "want." There's a big difference between the two, right?

As you think about protection, this verse promises that God will take care of you. Have you ever wondered how often God protects you that you don't even know about? He is blessing you and taking care of you every day. Often God brings what you need right at the last minute or even in ways you don't recognize at the time. The key is that He promises to protect you.

ChallengePoint

Trust is so important here. Do you trust God to take care of you? Really? Even if things look hopeless? Even if it seems as though He isn't paying any attention to you? Learn to trust Him as you seek His protection.

"The master was full of praise. 'Well done, my good and faithful servant. You have been faithful in handling this small amount, so now I will give you many more responsibilities. Let's celebrate together!'"

✳ MATTHEW 25:21

Doing the dirty work – the stuff no one else wants to do – isn't much fun. It's kind of a thankless job. At least, you might think that if you hadn't read this verse. The servant who was given the smallest amount of money in this story ended up with the most responsibility and the praise of his master. Why? Because he did a small job well.

Work hard at everything you do. You will definitely be noticed by God and He will reward you. Do a little thing for God, and then He will trust you with more.

ChallengePoint

You do understand that serving God is a privilege, don't you? It's amazing that God allows people to partner with Him in His work on this planet. If you work hard at the first small job God gives you, He will trust you with a bigger job the next time.

Knowing God by
Serving Him

But do not follow foolish stories that disagree with God's truth, but train yourself to serve God. Training your body helps you in some ways, but serving God helps you in every way by bringing you blessings in this life and in the future life, too.

* 1 TIMOTHY 4:7-8

How much information do you get from the Internet? If it is on the Internet it must be true, right? WRONG. Be careful what info you believe. You could easily be led astray. There are all kinds of twisted views of God, the Bible and the Christian life out there.

If you find something that doesn't agree with what you've heard before, run it by an adult you trust. Train yourself to serve God and God alone. Don't fall for fake versions of the Christian life.

ChallengePoint

Satan is sneaky. He can even use the Internet to confuse your faith. Be careful what you believe and be careful who you follow. Training to be more like God takes some effort. Make the effort though and you will be a better servant of God.

Knowing God by
Obeying Him

The good or bad that children do shows what they are like.

✳ PROVERBS 20:11

So what if you're rude to people? So what if you tell lies or cheat on tests? So what if you tell dirty jokes or talk back to your parents? You're just a kid so there is plenty of time for you to obey God and all that stuff when you're grown up, right? Never, ever say that it doesn't matter to God what you do or say just because you're a kid. It's not true.

God cares about your obedience from day one. From the minute you're born and the minute you accept Christ as Savior, He wants you to obey Him. It makes a difference in your relationship with Him – yes, even as a kid.

ChallengePoint

Here's something to think about – other kids your age may listen to what you say about God's love even more than they would listen to an adult. Remember, too, that they will be watching how you live to see if what you do matches what you say about your relationship with Him. Obeying and serving go together!

Knowing God by

Obeying Him

When people keep on sinning, it shows that they belong to the devil, who has been sinning since the beginning. But the Son of God came to destroy the works of the devil.

* 1 JOHN 3:8

It would be so much easier if you could just get an injection against sinning. You could get the injection at a certain age and that would take care of sinning for the rest of your life. OK, maybe you would need a booster at sixteen – the teen years are tough.

Too bad, though, that obeying is not a one-time thing. You can choose to obey one day and think you're doing pretty good … but then you have to do the same thing tomorrow and the next day and the next. If you don't choose to obey each day then you keep on sinning … just like the devil does. Obeying God, even wanting to obey Him, shows that you're in God's family. You belong to Him.

ChallengePoint

No injection available – obeying is up to you. The devil is going to do his best to keep you from obeying God, so you have to make a conscious choice several times a day to obey and not sin in order to show that you belong to God.

Knowing God by
Confessing Sin

Create in me a pure heart, O God, and renew a steadfast spirit within me.

✳ PSALM 51:10

Laundry is a necessary chore. Your mom or dad may do it right now, but the day will come when you have to learn how to do it for yourself. Clean clothes look nicer and smell better than dirty ones. Sometimes clothes are so dirty and stained that they need to be treated with special cleansers to get them clean.

Did you know that your heart gets dirty too? It is dirty because it's filled with sin and it has to be cleaned. How do you get it cleaned? You can't do it, but you can confess your sin to God – admit it. Tell Him you know that what you did was wrong. Then ask Him to clean your heart and help you be more obedient to Him. He will do the cleaning job.

ChallengePoint

Believe it or not, sometimes you may not even know what you need to confess. When that happens, ask God to show you what your sins are. That's a good way to learn where your weaknesses are so that you can ask God to help you in those areas.

Knowing God by
His Forgiveness

Yet now He has reconciled you to Himself through the death of Christ in His physical body. As a result, He has brought you into His own presence, and you are holy and blameless as you stand before Him without a single fault.

* COLOSSIANS 1:22

This is so awesome … did you notice the last part of this verse? It says you will stand before God WITHOUT A SINGLE FAULT. Every single sin you committed in your whole life will be forgiven and forgotten. God's forgiveness is total.

How many times do you think you've disobeyed God so far in your life? How many sins will you have committed by the time you are an old woman – like a million? Yeah, it's more than a few times. And yet, someday when you stand before God, He will not hold a single fault against you – not even one! When He forgives your sin, He also forgets it.

ChallengePoint

If only people could forgive like this, huh? God's forgiveness is a model for people to strive for. But remember that His complete forgiveness is possible because of Christ's death for your sins. That gift made it possible for you to be washed clean once you have asked Christ to be your Savior.

Knowing God by
Seeking His Guidance

Fools think they are doing right, but the wise listen to advice.

✳ PROVERBS 12:15

This is basic information. You may know someone who insists that her way of doing things is always right. She even makes others feel kind of foolish for wanting to do things their way instead of the way she says. A person who won't listen to the advice of others is a fool. The experiences and wisdom of others can be a big help to you in making decisions.

It is a sign of wisdom when a girl listens to others and learns from them. Of course, the best person to listen to is God. You can't go wrong by seeking guidance from Him.

ChallengePoint

You'll make few friends by insisting that your way is the only way. It's just arrogant. Remember that God sees the big picture of your whole life. He truly is the only One who knows what is best for you.

Understanding Anger

In the same way, the tongue is a small thing that makes grand speeches.

* JAMES 3:5

It's interesting that the biggest weapon of anger is the tongue. When you lose your temper you often end up saying mean things just to hurt the person you're mad at. Never a good idea. But the angry words spill out so quickly that it's hard to stop them.

Controlling what you say is so hard. You have to separate your anger from your words and that's really hard to do. However, looking at anger through the filter of God's command to love others means you better control what you say!

ChallengePoint

If you let anger take control of you, more than likely you will say things you'll regret later. Words come out that have no purpose other than to hurt other people. Those ugly words lie on a person's heart and hurt their self-image. There's no future in that and little evidence of God's love flowing from you. Watch it. Keep anger under control.

His Faithfulness

God, Your thoughts are precious to me. They are so many! If I could count them, they would be more than all the grains of sand. When I wake up, I am still with You.

⁎ PSALM 139:17-18

When you first start liking a particular guy he is on your mind constantly. It's hard to drag your mind to any other topic. Your thoughts are consumed with that one person and what he likes, what he's doing, and if he is thinking about you.

You don't have to wonder whether God is thinking about you. Seriously … walk along the beach and just think how many zillion grains of sand are on that beach. Can you even count them? No, don't even go there.

But look at all those grains of sand and think about this: God thinks about you more often than that number of grains of sand. That means you are NEVER out of His thoughts – NEVER!

ChallengePoint

God's faithfulness is shown in His constant thoughts about you. You are never out of His thoughts. Yep, that's faithfulness – He is committed to you by thinking about you all the time and caring about you every moment.

Knowing God by
Seeking Salvation

If anyone belongs to Christ, there is a new creation. The old things have gone; everything is made new!

* 2 CORINTHIANS 5:17

Makeovers are big these days. Reality shows on TV about makeovers with hairstyles, body image, clothing styles and even whole houses are big hits. Did you ever wish you could have a makeover? You could be taller, prettier or more stylish. Great idea, huh?

Well, you do get a makeover when you accept God's salvation. It changes everything for you. You become a new person when you ask Christ into your life. Your focus becomes obeying God and living for Him. The old you is gone!

ChallengePoint

Yahoo for makeovers! You can become a new person when you ask Christ into your life. He gets rid of the old self-centered stuff that made you disobedient to God. Your new life is focused on Him and being obedient, loving and willing to serve ... no matter what!

Knowing God by
Celebrating Him

Always be full of joy in the Lord. I say it again – rejoice!

* PHILIPPIANS 4:4

If you've ever been around a person who is always super-happy, you know that it can be very annoying. Sometimes you don't feel happy and you don't want to be around someone who thinks you should be!

Did you know that joy is different from happiness? Even so, this command to always be joyful may seem nearly impossible – ALWAYS be joyful? But since joy and happiness are two different things, it actually is possible.

This verse doesn't say to always be happy. Happiness is based on circumstances – what's going on in your life. Joy is based on trust. It's a state of mind because you know God is in control. You know you can trust Him and you know that He loves you, so you can always be joyful.

ChallengePoint

When you are full of joy in the Lord you can't help but celebrate Him. Just being in that state of mind reminds you of His amazing love for you. You'll constantly be thinking of all He does for you and how He cares for you. Those are all great things to celebrate!

Enduring

Three times I begged the Lord to make this suffering go away. But He replied, "My kindness is all you need. My power is strongest when you are weak." So if Christ keeps giving me His power, I will gladly brag about how weak I am.

✳ 2 CORINTHIANS 12:8-9

Change is not easy, regardless of what kind it is. Learning a new level of math. Perfecting a new skill in gymnastics. Moving and having to go to a new school and make new friends. Missing your dad after a divorce.

Any time you go through something painful, you may get to the point where you just beg God to take the pain away and let things be the way they used to be. The apostle Paul knew what that was like – but he had the endurance to keep on going, and God blessed him by giving him the strength to keep on going.

ChallengePoint

The apostle Paul found his endurance in God's strength. He trusted God to give him the power he needed. It's only when things are tough that you find out if you have the strength and power to endure. If you call on God for strength to keep on going, He will give it and you will be blessed.

Let your roots grow down into Him, and let your lives be built on Him. Then your faith will grow strong in the truth you were taught, and you will overflow with thankfulness.

✱ COLOSSIANS 2:7

Did you know that you have roots? Kind of weird, huh? Roots in this verse could also be called your foundation – it is the beginning of where your strength comes from. Tree roots go deep into the earth and get the nutrition and water the tree needs to grow.

In the same way, if your roots go down deep into Christ, your nutrition and water will come from Him. That means you'll be feeding your spirit and your heart with healthy stuff that teaches you to obey God and live for Him. Christ wants to help you grow strong in your faith. He will do whatever you will allow Him to do to help you.

ChallengePoint

To learn to be more like Christ, your roots must grow in Him. Your nutrition must come from Him. God wants the best for you and that will come from letting Christ be your food and water. Learn to be like Him by learning from Him.

Knowing God by
Being Like Christ

Keep on loving each other as brothers. Do not forget to entertain strangers, for by so doing some people have entertained angels without knowing it. Remember those in prison as if you were their fellow prisoners, and those who are mistreated as if yourselves were suffering.

* HEBREWS 13:1-3

The hardest lesson to learn at your age is sometimes this one: Life is not all about you. Some kids live like everything is all about them. They are most concerned about how a situation affects them and don't care much what happens to others.

Thinking outside yourself is the beginning of being like Christ. Loving others and being kind – even to strangers – and paying attention to people who are in trouble.

That means spending time with those who are sort of undesirable – people you might not choose to associate with; people who are dirty, sick or in trouble. Those kinds of people never bothered Christ. He loved them all.

ChallengePoint

Becoming more like Christ means thinking of others and their needs before your own. It means getting out of your comfort zone and becoming friends with people who are way different from you. Can you do that?

Knowing God by
Loving Him

Be very careful to obey all the commands and the instructions that Moses gave to you. Love the LORD your God, walk in all His ways, obey His commands, hold firmly to Him, and serve Him with all your heart and all your soul.

✳ JOSHUA 22:5

Imagine jumping in a swimming pool and trying to keep your hair dry. It is a nuisance to get it wet and have to do it all over again. But holding your head above water and protecting it from splashes is a nuisance too. Yeah, it makes swimming not so much fun. Pretty much all you can do is stand there, protecting your hair. You can't do much in the water if you're trying to keep your hair dry.

Well, it's the same way with God's love – if you're not going to jump in with both feet and let your whole body love Him back, then all you're doing is standing in a pool of water.

ChallengePoint

Go ahead ... get your hair wet! God loves you completely. Love Him back completely. Don't hold anything back.

Knowing God by
His Love

The Lord disciplines those He loves, and He punishes everyone He accepts as His child.

* HEBREWS 12:6

Your parents may say that when they have to punish you it hurts them more than it hurts you. You probably think, "Yeah, right." Well, believe it or not, it's true. It's also true of God. He doesn't enjoy punishing you, but He does it because He loves you.

Punished because of love? Does that confuse you? Look, if He didn't care at all about whether you learn and mature, then He wouldn't bother with punishing you. He'd just let you do whatever. But He does care. You are His child and He loves you. So He wants you to learn lessons that will help you mature.

* ChallengePoint

Granted, being punished is not fun. But if you can view God's discipline and punishment as what He does because He loves you and wants to help you become a stronger Christian, does that make it easier? Unfortunately, being punished is about the best way you learn. So, thank God for caring enough to punish you.

Knowing God by
Showing Courage

So do not be ashamed to tell people about our Lord Jesus, and do not be ashamed of me, in prison for the Lord. But suffer with me for the Good News. God, who gives us the strength to do that, saved us and made us His holy people.

* 2 TIMOTHY 1:8-9

Honesty time: Do you have some friends who have no clue that you go to church or read devotional books? You don't want them to know because they might make fun of you. You are … ashamed.

Courage shows the depth of your commitment. In other words, if your belief in God is deep and strong, you'll be courageous in telling others about it. You won't be ashamed to take a stand for Him. Your courage can come from God's strength. He'll give you the power you need. Be sure, though, 'cause life can get tough sometimes when you take a stand for Him.

ChallengePoint

There's no riding the fence on your commitment to Christ. Be courageous and take a stand for God. When you do, expect to pay for it – Satan will want to slow you down. But turn to God for strength and even more courage! He will give it to you.

Knowing God by
Witnessing His Power

The voice of the LORD echoes above the sea. The God of glory thunders. The LORD thunders over the mighty sea. The voice of the LORD is powerful; the voice of the LORD is majestic.

* PSALM 29:3-4

A group of guys playing together can get really loud, can't they? Guys are … different. They often like to be loud and a little wild. In your opinion, does loud mean powerful? Not necessarily, but loud sure gets people's attention, doesn't it?

Look at how God's power is described – His voice is louder than the sea. It's powerful and full of majesty. That sounds like it commands attention. It sounds as though God's voice shows His power. You'd probably listen when you heard it.

ChallengePoint

Don't get the impression that God's power is only seen in loud stuff. It is not seen only in things such as thunderstorms or massive waterfalls. It's seen in the miracle of a newborn baby and in the simplicity of a flower. God's voice is powerful and the entire world will listen when He speaks. One day everyone will fall to their knees at the sound of His voice. Do you honor His power right now?

Knowing God by
Abiding in Him

The world and everything that people want in it are passing away, but the person who does what God wants lives forever.

✻ 1 JOHN 2:17

Wow, if you pay attention to what the world tells you is important, you'll be grabbing for money, fame, power, popularity, fancy stuff, lots of gadgets … the world tells you that you NEED a lot of stuff. What are you grabbing on to? Where do you spend your time? What is most important to you? What do you want most in this world?

If each of those questions had an answer other than "Living for God" then you've got a problem. Living for God and obeying Him by sticking close to Him is abiding in Him. That should be most important in your life.

ChallengePoint

God lasts forever. God's children will live forever with Him. Nothing else in this world will last into eternity. Only God. Stick close to Him. Make Him the most important thing in your life. In the end that's all you will have.

Trusting Him

You make our hearts glad because we trust You, the only God.

✻ PSALM 33:21

Knowing you can trust someone is an amazing thing. Trust gives you a confidence in the person's support and friendship. It gives you peace in problems because the person you trust will be there for you.

Hopefully there are some people in your life whom you can trust. But the person you can trust the most and always depend on without a doubt is God.

What that means is that trusting God completely gives you the freedom to feel real joy and peace. You know you don't have to worry about anything, because you can trust Him. So relax and rejoice.

ChallengePoint

Don't get discouraged about the subject of trust. It does not come easily. It's a process to learn to trust God all the time, in any situation. But look at the joy that comes from trusting. That makes it worth starting the process, right?

Knowing God by
His Love

"I loved you as the Father loved Me. Now remain in My love."

✳ JOHN 15:9

Everyone wants to be loved and have someone to love. It seems like a simple thing to desire. After all, the Bible is filled with stories of God's love. It leaves no doubt that God has amazing love for His Son, Jesus. He loved Jesus enough to raise Him back to life after He was killed. He had a plan for Jesus' life and that shows His love.

Well, Jesus loves you as much as God loves Him. His love for you is the reason He followed God's plan for Him! Jesus passes the love along to you by teaching, guiding and protecting you. He encourages you to stay close to Him and enjoy His love.

ChallengePoint

How cool – everyone IS loved and DOES have someone to love! God's love is bottomless. He loves you more than you can imagine. Stay close to Him – enjoy His love.

Knowing God by
Praying

So let us come boldly to the throne of our gracious God. There we will receive His mercy, and we will find grace to help us when we need it most.

∗ HEBREWS 4:16

When you have to go up and talk to your teacher, are you brave and outspoken or are you meek and quiet? Sometimes it is scary to talk to someone in authority. You may not be sure how your requests will be received.

Never fear, you can come boldly to God with your requests because you know without a doubt that He loves you. You know He wants the best for you. It is so amazing that God wants to hear your requests. He wants to forgive your sins. He wants to help you in your life. You don't have to beg Him. You don't have to sneak up on Him. You don't have to be shy about talking with Him.

ChallengePoint

Prayer is such a privilege. Use it boldly and come to God with your praises and your requests. He loves you and wants you to come to Him.

Knowing God by
Seeking His Protection

Cast your cares on the Lord and He will sustain you; He will never let the righteous fall.

✳ Psalm 55:22

When you have a problem you probably tell your friends about it. They listen to your worries and feel great sympathy for you. But your friends can't fix the problem. They can't really do anything except listen to you. That's helpful, but it would be nice to have someone who can actually protect you in the middle of a problem.

Guess what? You do have someone who cares enough to listen to your problems and who has the power to protect you! God! He has power over everything and … He loves you.

ChallengePoint

God promises to take care of the godly. That means He will take care of those people who love, trust and seek to obey Him. Take steps along that pathway and then give your problems to God. He will take care of you. He promises.

Do what the Lord wants, and He will
give you your heart's desire.

~ PSALM 37:4

October

Knowing God by
Serving Him

O Lord, You are my God; I will exalt You and praise Your name, for in perfect faithfulness You have done marvelous things, things planned long ago.

* Isaiah 25:1

Famous people such as movie stars, athletes and musicians usually have fan clubs. Groups of kids like this individual so much that they are happy to be identified as a fan. A fan plasters her room with posters of her hero, visits the fan website, wears shirts advertising her hero's name and anything else she can think of.

Are you a fan of God? If you love Him and serve Him, you are. A fan of God will praise Him by saying out loud how awesome He is and what incredible things He does. A fan of God uses her life to honor Him by making choices in how she lives and how she speaks that will show others that she respects Him and desires to obey Him.

ChallengePoint

Hopefully you are serving God by being His fan. Serving God is a journey. Some days you will succeed. Some days you will fail. But keep moving in the direction of serving God with your voice and your life.

Knowing God by
Serving Him

Be holy in all you do, just as God, the One who called you, is holy.

✳ 1 PETER 1:15

This is kind of a scary command, isn't it? Be holy? What does that mean? Holy means "to be set apart." So, if you're holy you are set apart from the rest of the world in order to do God's work. You have a different purpose than people who do not know God.

Serving God by being holy means being willing to do whatever God wants – regardless of what people around you are doing.

ChallengePoint

OK, admittedly this is not always easy. Your friends may give you a hard time when you don't want to do stuff they do. They may make fun of you. They may question you. Ultimately, they will notice that serving God is the most important thing in your life. That's a good thing.

Knowing God by
Obeying Him

Oh, the joys of those who do not follow the advice of the wicked, or stand around with sinners, or join in with mockers.

* PSALM 1:1

Do you want joy in your life? Remember the difference between joy and happiness? Happiness is based on circumstances and changes with the wind. Joy comes from deep inside and comes from a confident trust in God.

This is what this verse teaches about joy:

1. Obeying God is the most important thing.
2. Obeying God is not going to happen if you take advice from people who don't care about Him.
3. If you hang out with people who don't care about God, you probably won't care about Him either and then will not obey God.
4. Don't hang out with people who don't obey God.

ChallengePoint

Well, it can't get any simpler than that, can it? Obeying God is a choice you make every day (many times a day in fact). Get your advice about life from people who obey God. That's the only way you'll keep going in that direction.

Knowing God by
Obeying Him

From heaven God shows how angry He is with all the wicked and evil things that sinful people do to crush the truth.

✳ ROMANS 1:18

Have you ever stood up to another girl who was trying to get everyone to do something wrong? It takes courage to stand up to someone who is powerful and wants everyone to do what she says. It takes courage to stand for God. It's worth it though.

Remember this, God is not wishy-washy. Yes, He loves you. Yes, He wants the best for you. Yes, He gives second, third, fourth and fiftieth chances for obedience. But He has a bottom line. When someone's actions of disobedience shuts down the truth being shared with others, God gets angry … and He shows it. You don't want to see that.

ChallengePoint

No, you don't want God's anger to be directed at you. God is patient and He gives many chances for obedience. But He gets angry if your disobedience causes others to be unable to hear the truth of His love. So, if you need to be courageous in obeying Him … do it.

Knowing God by
Obeying Him

In the same way, faith by itself – that does nothing – is dead.

　　　　　　　　　　* JAMES 2:17

If you lived alone in a cave, a zillion miles from everyone else, then trusting God alone and not doing anything might be enough. But you don't live that way. There are people all around you who need to know about God's love.

So, yeah, trusting God is important. Believing He loves you is important. But this isn't enough to be considered obedience. Your faith needs to show in your life by the things you do and the words you speak. You can say all the "churchy" words you know, but if your actions don't match your words, you are not obeying. Get busy – do something.

ChallengePoint

There are people all around you who need to know that God loves them and you love them. That takes action. Don't bother spouting Bible verses or speaking "churchy" words if your actions are not matching. The two need to go together – your words of faith and your actions. That shows real obedience.

Knowing God by
Confessing Sin

Confess your sins to each other and pray for each other so God can heal you. When a believing person prays, great things happen.

＊ JAMES 5:16

Confession means honesty and accountability. That's why God tells you to confess your sins to other people.

Granted, it's not easy to come clean with another person, but think about this: Confessing to another person builds a family relationship. That person can hold you accountable to not keep sinning the same sins. She can pray for you and encourage you.

ChallengePoint

Of course, you don't go around confessing your sins to any Joe Schmo you meet. It's important to choose a mature Christian who can give you good advice and who will actually seriously pray for you. Your friend may confess to you, too, so you can pray for her. The Christian life is not meant to be lived alone. God wants people to help each other.

Knowing God by
His Forgiveness

Even before He made the world, God loved us and chose us in Christ to be holy and without fault in His eyes.

* EPHESIANS 1:4

Making up your mind about something before you have all the facts is not a good thing. It often means that you make judgments which are not fair.

However, God made up His mind about something before He even made the world. That's right, His mind was made up long before you were even born. God had already decided that when you asked for His forgiveness, He would give it. Before He even made the world, He had already decided that you were His child. He loved you before you even came to be!

So, whatever you throw at Him now, He will forgive … because He loves you.

ChallengePoint

Wow, God has loved you for a long time. He decided a long time ago to forgive you! This gives you confidence in Him, doesn't it? You know that there will be times when you mess up. There will even be times when you choose to disobey (bad choice by the way), but God has already forgiven you. Wow … that's love!

Knowing God by
Seeking His Guidance

You know where I go and where I lie down. You know everything I do.

✳ PSALM 139:3

You've played hide-and-seek, haven't you? If you find a really good hiding place then the "it" person can't find you. Did you know that you can never hide from God? He always knows where you are and what you're doing.

The awesome thing is that God has a plan for your life. He has a plan for what you do, where you go to school, who you marry, where you live and what your future job is. Do you find that comforting, or scary? Don't be scared, remember, He loves you so His plan will make you happy and be the absolute best for you.

ChallengePoint

God knows everything about you, but how do you find out what God's plan for you is? Ask Him. Read His Word and pray. Try to pay attention to the opportunities you get and notice what you really, really enjoy doing. He'll guide you 'cause He wants you to know.

Knowing God by
Understanding Anger

Those who bring trouble on their families inherit the wind. The fool will be a servant to the wise.

* PROVERBS 11:29

How well do you get along with your brothers and sisters? Come on, be honest. If you have brothers or sisters, the answer is probably that you fight with them once in a while. What about your parents? How do you get along with them? Do you sometimes feel they are unfair? Do you sometimes argue with them?

It makes sense when you think about it – you live with them, share space with them and are most comfortable letting your feelings show with family. But God says to control that anger. Don't bring trouble on your family by letting your anger run free. That would make you look foolish.

ChallengePoint

What does "inherit the wind" mean? It means you are left with nothing. Everything that really matters is blown away by your anger. If you have anger issues ask God to help you control it and help you be patient and forgiving with your family.

Knowing God by
His Faithfulness

Jesus Christ is the same yesterday, today, and forever.

✳ HEBREWS 13:8

Moods are the worst. You know how hard it is to deal with your friend when she's in a lousy mood. Some girls are so moody that you don't know from one day to the next if you're going to get "nice friend" or "psycho friend." It's tiring.

You can really appreciate that Jesus is the same all the time. You will never have to worry about His bad moods or grumpiness. He is always the same. That's a comfort, isn't it? You can always know what He expects and what He wants. You can always know that He loves you … no matter what … and that He wants the best for you.

ChallengePoint

Sometimes Jesus is described as an anchor in life – an anchor holds a boat in place. Jesus is your anchor. He holds you in place. He is steady and you can depend on Him … always.

Knowing God by
Seeking Salvation

"Therefore, whoever humbles himself like this child is the greatest in the kingdom of heaven."

✳ MATTHEW 18:4

How cool is this? Did you ever think you would hear God say that grown-ups should be like children? Well, here you are – this verse is proof.

Why does God say this? Because in seeking salvation it's important to understand that you've done nothing to deserve it; you didn't earn it. A child who isn't filled up with ideas about her own importance is more likely to feel that way than an adult.

ChallengePoint

Yay! Something that kids do better than adults! Keep your childlike humility as you seek salvation and growing in your faith. You've done nothing to deserve the gifts God gives. But your humility makes you great in His eyes.

Knowing God by
Being Thankful

Enter His gates with thanksgiving; go into His courts with praise. Give thanks to Him and praise His name.

* PSALM 100:4

Do you have a happy dance? You know – that thing you do when you're so happy you can't even find words to express it.

Have you ever done your happy dance for God? Why does the Bible tell you to be thankful to God? Because when you take time to think about all He does for you and gives you, it helps you see how much He loves you.

Then there's kind of a building effect – a little bit of thankfulness becomes a little bit more, then a little bit more. Thanksgiving grows into praise and pretty soon you're doing your happy dance!

ChallengePoint

What are you thankful for right this moment? Think about it. When you come up with one thing, then think of a second and a third. You will see your thankfulness grow into praise.

Knowing God by
Celebrating Him

And they were calling to one another: "Holy, holy, holy is the LORD Almighty; the whole earth is full of His glory."

* ISAIAH 6:3

Have you ever been speechless? Have you ever been so blown away by some important person or surprised by something that you couldn't find any words to say?

Do you ever wonder how you will act when you see God? Will you be so awed that you can't utter a word? Will you fall to your knees in praise? Or maybe, like the people in this Scripture verse, you will just start celebrating Him by shouting out how awesome and holy He is! How cool would that be?

ChallengePoint

It's kind of fun to think what your automatic response to God might be – how you will react without even thinking. There's no doubt that it's going to be amazing to stand in God's presence. AMAZING. Whatever your response is, you will be celebrating Him and who He is! It will be a party of praise!

Knowing God by
Enduring

We also pray that you will be strengthened with all His glorious power so you will have all the endurance and patience you need. May you be filled with joy, always thanking the Father. He has enabled you to share in the inheritance that belongs to His people, who live in the light.

✳ COLOSSIANS 1:11-12

In order to endure, you have to stop thinking about yourself. You must stop thinking about how tired or hungry you are, how hot it is or if your hands are dirty. To endure in God's work, you must think about the people you are serving and how important God's work is.

Think of a marathon runner. Her body is able to endure a 26.3 mile race because she trains her muscles by constant practice. She feeds her body the right nutrition it needs to endure. In your Christian life you need to do the same. Strengthen your heart and soul with God's power. That's the only way to endure through whatever life brings you.

ChallengePoint

God wants you to endure and be filled with joy at the same time. There is satisfaction in finishing well. There is joy in endurance through Christ's power.

Knowing God by
Being Like Christ

It makes a lot of sense to be a person of few words and to stay calm.

✳ PROVERBS 17:27

Calm? Seriously? Obviously the writer of Proverbs didn't know your family. He didn't know your friends or how hard they are to get along with sometimes. He didn't know a lot about your life! He couldn't have or he wouldn't have told you to stay calm!

Why did the writer of Proverbs put these two things together: use few words and be calm? Because a person who loses her temper usually ends up saying things she doesn't mean; things that hurt other people. Living like Christ means not doing that. Be smart and know when to be quiet.

ChallengePoint

✳ This is such great advice: Keep your temper under control. Think about the words you say and how they will make other people feel. Be like Christ. Be wise.

"Be compassionate, just as your Father is compassionate."

* LUKE 6:36

Being compassionate takes a lot of energy. It means caring about others and their problems. Their problems pile on top of your own problems and it's exhausting! Compassion means caring about others' problems over your own, and that's hard!

When you read this verse, did you think, "I don't have the energy to be compassionate"? Slow down, being compassionate just means caring about other people. Caring about their problems, their worries, their fears. Even if you can't "fix" them, you can show people that you care. Caring … just as you want others to care about you.

ChallengePoint

Christ is your example. He cared about other people. He often helped them with their problems. Even if you can't actually help someone, you can pray for them. Show that you are compassionate, like Christ, by praying for others.

Knowing God by
Being Like Christ

Serving God does make us very rich, if we are satisfied with what we have. We brought nothing into the world, so we can take nothing out.

✳ 1 TIMOTHY 6:6-7

Contentment is not of this world. What that means is that the world – TV, magazines, movies and people – will always tell you that you need more and more stuff. Some people spend all their energy and strength trying to get more "stuff." They seem to think that the girl with the most stuff wins the game of life. Not true.

If you spend all your time and energy working to get money to buy stuff that you have to take care of, but you ignore your relationship with God and even ignore other people – you lose.

ChallengePoint

Contentment is Christlike. Being like Christ means building a strong relationship with God and paying attention to people. That's all that really matters. When life on this earth ends you can't take any "stuff" with you to heaven, so don't worry about it. Spend your energy on what really matters.

Knowing God by
Loving Others

"The second command is this: 'Love your neighbor as you love yourself.' There are no commands more important than these."

✳ MARK 12:31

Do you love yourself? You might answer "No" right away. But stop and think about it. You take care of your body by feeding it and getting rest. You protect yourself. You may not always be proud of yourself, but you do love yourself.

When Jesus gave this command, He had just gotten through saying that the first commandment is to love God with all your heart, all your soul, all your mind, and all your strength. He followed that up with these words.

Loving others is just as important as loving God. Did you get that? It's JUST AS important as loving God. That's amazing.

ChallengePoint

Yes, you do love yourself and you should love others. This verse leaves no doubt about how God feels about how you treat other people. Love them. Get your own ego and agenda out of the way and just care for others.

Knowing God by
Showing Love

Love isn't selfish or quick tempered. It doesn't keep a record of wrongs that others do.

✳ 1 CORINTHIANS 13:5

Do you keep a mental list of all the things your friends or family do to you? You say you forgive them for these things, but you keep a list tucked away in the back of your mind so that if a person slights you again, you can quickly remind her of previous things she has done to you.

Hmm, you've probably heard that once God forgives your sins, He wipes them out of His memory. That's unlike your list of remembered wrongs, isn't it? God's love – true love – doesn't demand its own way. He wants you to love and serve Him because you want to, not because you have to. His love isn't irritable because He's tired or moody. And … it wipes away all wrongs.

ChallengePoint

God's true love forgives and forgets. That's the model, though it's not easy to do. Ask God to teach you to love others the way He loves you.

Knowing God by
Showing Courage

The eternal God is your refuge, and His everlasting arms are under you.

✳ DEUTERONOMY 33:27

A mom and dad of a toddler who is learning to walk watch their little one so closely. Any time the baby gets close to falling, mom or dad's arms are there to catch her. Of course, babies have very little fear because they don't understand falling … and they know Mom and Dad will be close by.

Being courageous would be easy if you absolutely-without-a-doubt knew that you couldn't be hurt and couldn't lose. Well, you CAN know that because God promises to be your refuge – the place you can hide from your enemies. His strong arms are always under you to catch you when you fall.

ChallengePoint

This verse doesn't mean you won't have problems – you will. It doesn't mean you won't hurt sometimes – you will. But it does mean that God is always with you and He won't let you have problems or pain so terrible that you can't recover. His arms will catch you.

Knowing God by
Witnessing His Power

He will destroy death forever. The LORD God will wipe away every tear from every face. He will take away the shame of His people from the earth. The LORD has spoken.

* ISAIAH 25:8

Death is a difficult part of life. Losing someone you love hurts very much. But there's comfort in the fact that one day God is going to win. That's the bottom line. Whatever junk is going on in this world – whatever battles it seems like Satan is winning – it will all eventually end and God will win the war.

He will defeat death because His children will be able to live forever. He will win over everything done and said against His work.

ChallengePoint

Wow! God is going to win. He's going to defeat everything – even death! And His power is available to you. He loves you so His power works for you, protects you and guides you. How awesome is that?

Knowing God by
Abiding in Him

I ask only one thing from the LORD. This is what I want: Let me live in the LORD's house all my life. Let me see the LORD's beauty and look with my own eyes at His Temple.

* PSALM 27:4

What do you think about this prayer? Would you ask if you could be with God always? Would you be happy obeying Him and thinking about Him forever?

Seriously – would you be willing to pray this prayer? It would mean abiding with Him (being close to Him all the time) … doing what He commands (obeying Him) … not doing what the other girls – who don't care a bit about God – sometimes think is fun.

ChallengePoint

Asking to always be in God's presence is really kind of weird because He has already told you that He is always with you. So, He knows what you're doing, thinking and saying all the time. All the time. This prayer then is for you to be aware that God is close by you.

Knowing God by
His Love

And this hope will never disappoint us, because God has poured out His love to fill our hearts. He gave us His love through the Holy Spirit, whom God has given to us.

✳ ROMANS 5:5

Is the Holy Spirit kind of a mystery to you? Yeah, it's hard to understand how God is three Persons and yet only one Person. The important thing to understand though is that God, the Holy Spirit, lives in your heart.

How do you know? He's that little urge you sometimes feel to do the right thing. He's the gentle voice in your mind that warns you about a bad choice. God gave you the Holy Spirit to live in your heart because He loves you. The Holy Spirit is God's presence with you always.

ChallengePoint

The Holy Spirit was sent to earth when Jesus went back to heaven. He is God's presence – His gift of love to His children. Pay attention to His guidance and direction in your heart.

Knowing God by
His Love

"For God loved the world so much that He gave His one and only Son, so that everyone who believes in Him will not perish but have eternal life."

* JOHN 3:16

God's gift of Jesus is greater than any other gift you have ever received. Why? Because most gifts are purchased and just cost money. The gift of Jesus was a gift of love.

God gave His own Son – His only Son – because He loves you. He sent Jesus to earth, knowing that He was not going to be treated well. It was going to be tough for Him. People would treat Him badly and then kill Him.

It is because of Jesus' death and His resurrection (His victory over death) that you can have a real relationship with God!

ChallengePoint

That's how much God loves you. His love cost Him something precious. He probably could have come up with another plan for you to be able to go to heaven. But this one cost Him something, so it shows you how much He loves you.

Knowing God by
Praying

*Depend on the Lord; trust Him, and He will take care of you.
Then your goodness will shine like the sun, and your fairness like
the noonday sun.*

* PSALM 37:5-6

Prayer is conversation with God. It's amazing that God Himself wants you to talk with Him. He wants to hear what's on your mind. He wants to hear your dreams. He's happy to hear your requests. God wants to guide and direct your life with His standards and values.

But how can you expect God to help you if you don't talk to Him? Tell Him what you're facing, whether it's a difficult test, a big game, a concert, a problem with a friend or trouble in your family. Commit it to Him – trust Him to take care of it and to help you through it.

ChallengePoint

Be realistic – this doesn't mean God will instantly wipe away the problem or difficulty you have. It means He will be with you and strengthen you to get through it. You will be in a better place because you trusted Him.

Surely Your goodness and unfailing love will pursue me all the days of my life, and I will live in the house of the LORD forever.

* PSALM 23:6

A student who is a really good athlete will often be pursued by various colleges offering scholarships or other special perks if she will choose to attend their college and play her sport for them.

It feels really good to be wanted. Did you know that you're being pursued too? God's love is pursuing you – moving around behind you and guiding you into safety with Him. He loves you and wants to protect you.

ChallengePoint

All of God's children are being pursued by Him. Some people think they know what's best for them, but they really don't. Let God guide, direct and shepherd you into safety through His love.

Knowing God by
Seeking His Protection

"Don't be afraid. I am with you. Don't tremble with fear. I am your God. I will make you strong, as I protect you with My arm and give you victories."

* ISAIAH 41:10

Maybe you have had to find your way around a brand-new school all by yourself. Kinda scary, huh? If you're in an unfamiliar place and you don't know which way to go, you might be scared. You don't know how to find your way out and you don't know if the place where you are is dangerous.

God reminds you that you can trust Him to always be with you, so you're never completely alone. He says you don't have to be afraid because He is always with you.

ChallengePoint

So, will God help you find yourself around the school? He might send you a new friend who can help you. Take courage in God's presence with you. If you become frightened and a little discouraged, stop and remind yourself that God is with you and will always, always help you.

Knowing God by
Serving Him

So put all evil things out of your life: sexual sinning, doing evil, letting evil thoughts control you, wanting things that are evil, and greed. This is really serving a false god.

* COLOSSIANS 3:5

Do you have secrets? Yeah, everyone does. Are some of your secrets things that you really don't want anyone else to know about because you aren't sure what others would think of you if they knew about them?

Well, you can hide things from others (yeah, even your parents) but you cannot hide them from God. The places you visit on the Internet – He sees. The movies and TV shows you watch – He knows about. The jokes you and your friends tell – He hears. Are you embarrassed to know what He knows about you?

ChallengePoint

Don't get caught up in the junk of this world and think it's more important than God. It isn't. Nothing is more important than serving and honoring Him; even though it makes you "different" from the other kids sometimes. It's worth it.

Knowing God by
Obeying Him

Choose today whom you will serve ... but as for me and my family, we will serve the Lord.

✳ Joshua 24:15

How you live every day is a choice. Your choice. You can take a stand of choosing to serve God, even if your friends are not choosing that. Be courageous and take a stand. Show some backbone. Be brave. Those are some phrases that come to mind with this verse.

Decide if you're going to obey God. Decide ... because if you don't decide, then you are deciding you aren't going to obey Him. Get it? Not to decide is to decide. There's no middle of the road here. Choose to obey God.

ChallengePoint

Yep, no middle of the road. Don't think you're going to wait to decide for God when you're older – do that and you're making a choice right now. Choose today, and every day, to serve God.

Knowing God by
Obeying Him

LORD, we are waiting for Your way of justice. Our souls want to remember You and Your name.

✷ ISAIAH 26:8

Do you trust God? Really trust Him? Do you trust Him to bring about fair judgments, regardless of the situation? Bottom line: If you aren't obeying God, then you aren't trusting Him. If you aren't trusting Him then you aren't glorifying Him.

Obeying is the foundation for all the other things to be built on. God wants your obedience, trust and glory to be given to Him.

ChallengePoint

The bottom line of this is the question: What does God really mean to your life? You can "say" you love Him and trust Him, but if you aren't obeying Him ... then all those "words" are just lies.

Knowing God by
Being Faithful

God will bless you, if you don't give up when your faith is being tested. He will reward you with a glorious life, just as He rewards everyone who loves Him.

* JAMES 1:12

It's really hard to celebrate when you have problems in your life. How do you say thanks when someone you love gets really sick? Think about what it takes to make your muscles stronger. By working them hard, right? When you exercise and work your muscles they get stronger and can work longer and harder.

Your faith is like that too. It's through the hard times that it grows. It is during problems that you learn God will take care of you, that He will help and strengthen you.

ChallengePoint

Faith doesn't really grow in easy times, because you don't really need to see that God is protecting you, guiding you and loving you then. When you have problems, you see that God is with you and taking care of you. Your faith grows a little stronger each time you see that.

Today is a gift. That's why it is called the present.

~ ANONYMOUS

November

Knowing God by
Seeking Salvation

He saved us, not because of the righteous things we had done, but because of His mercy. He washed away our sins, giving us a new birth and new life through the Holy Spirit.

✳ TITUS 3:5

Look at the salvation plan:

What are you saved from?

1. Your sins – the nasty, mean, evil and selfish things you think, say and do.
2. Hell – separation from God forever and ever.

What are you saved for?

1. A friendship and relationship with God.
2. Heaven – being with God forever.

ChallengePoint

✳ Have you made the choice for salvation? Salvation is as simple as asking Jesus to be your Savior, forgive your sin, and live in your heart.

Give thanks to the LORD and pray to Him. Tell the nations what He has done.

✳ 1 CHRONICLES 16:8

Thanksgiving is a great holiday celebrated at various times in different countries. It's a great time for families to gather and usually have a celebration dinner and actually tell each other what things in their lives they are thankful for.

Why is it important to say thanks out loud? God appreciates being thanked for what He does. He doesn't want thanks just for the sake of thanks though. Saying thanks makes you think about how much God loves you.

Thinking about what to thank Him for makes you think about all He does. Also, sharing your thanks with others celebrates God's work in the world.

ChallengePoint

Take time to thank God for all He does for you. Tell others about His love, His kindness and His gifts.

Knowing God by
Celebrating Him

Make a joyful symphony before the LORD! Let the sea and every-thing in it shout His praise.

* PSALM 98:6-7

Jesus once said that if people didn't shout praise to Him, the rocks along the road would. Did you know that creation shouts God's praise all the time?

It's true! When the ocean waves crash to the shore they are saying, "Praise God who created us!" When a tiny flower pushes up through the soil, it is praising God's strength and power. When the wind ripples through the high branches of a tree, it's celebrating God's gentleness. When the sun rises every morning and sets every evening it is celebrating God's constant work. Creation praises Him every day.

ChallengePoint

Is it kind of weird to think that the things you naturally expect to happen in nature are really songs of praise to God? OK, but what or who makes those "normal" things happen? God does. So, nature sings back its praise to Him. Do you do the same?

Knowing God by
Being Like Christ

"For where your treasure is, there your heart will be also."

✳ MATTHEW 6:21

Do you understand what this verse is saying? It's very important ... what is most important to you? What is your "treasure"? It's important to know that because you will find that you're spending a lot of time on that one thing. Whether its friends or a hobby, it will take a lot of your thoughts and energy. That will impact how important God is in your life.

What you spend most of your thoughts and energy on is REALLY what's most important to you.

ChallengePoint

So, you have to make a decision – is living for Christ important to you? If it is, then your thoughts, prayers, time and energy will be directed toward learning how to do that. If it isn't, then you will not spend much time on it. Hobbies and friends are OK, but they should never be more important to you than knowing God.

Knowing God by
Loving Others

We don't need to write to you about the importance of loving each other, for God Himself has taught you to love one another.

* 1 THESSALONIANS 4:9

Do you have a lot of homework? Some teachers give so much homework that their students come home from school and start right in on their homework and don't finish until bedtime. Homework and school become a full-time job. So, when you hear that God has lessons for you, too, it may not make you very happy.

However, when you get a lesson from God, you'd better pay attention. God says over and over in His Word that it's important to Him that people love one another. It's not good enough to just love your family and friends. It's not even good enough to love people who are a lot like you. God says to love your enemies and those who think and live differently than you do.

ChallengePoint

It's easiest to love people who are like you. It's a little hard to love people who are a bit different from you. It's really hard to love people who are super-different. It's almost impossible to love your enemies. It's the hard thing to do, but it's the right thing to do.

Knowing God by
Giving

God can bless you with everything you need, and you will always have more than enough to do all kinds of good things for others.

✳ 2 CORINTHIANS 9:8

Do you have a lot of stuff? Do you have enough stuff? Do you have just what you need? Do you not have what you need? Do you see the progression in those questions? God gives some people a lot. They have nice homes, lots of toys, clothes, food and, well, just stuff. Other people do not have homes or enough food to eat or clothes to wear.

Have you ever thought that God gives you stuff so you can share with others? If you have two of something, give one to someone who has none. Get it? God does not give stuff to you to make you wealthy. He gives so you can help those who do not have enough to live.

ChallengePoint

The world is filled with people who don't have homes, enough food to eat, shoes, backpacks for their kids, medicine ... and on and on. God says it is the responsibility of those who have plenty to help those who do not have enough. Research how you can do that.

Knowing God by
Suppressing Our Pride

And this is the reason: God lives forever and is holy. He is high and lifted up. He says, "I live in a high and holy place, but I also live with people who are sad and humble. I give new life to those who are humble and to those whose hearts are broken."

✳ Isaiah 57:15

The girl who prances around at school like she's the queen … is not. She may be super important in her own mind, and even try to command respect from all of you, but this verse shows she's got it all backwards. What kind of person is truly important? Look who lives close to God … those who are humble.

Pride gets you nowhere in God's eyes. A person who is humble is more likely to be repentant of her sins and willing to submit to God. It makes her more loving and encouraging to others too. That makes a person more like God and that's the goal, right?

ChallengePoint

God repeatedly puts much importance on the command to love others. It's not really possible to be filled with pride in yourself, bragging about yourself, and also be encouraging and supportive to others. God is much more pleased with humility – it allows you to focus on others.

Knowing God by
Trusting Him

You love Him even though you have never seen Him. Though you do not see Him now, you trust Him; and you rejoice with a glorious, inexpressible joy.

✳ 1 PETER 1:8

It's so sad when a good friend moves away. Of course you promise to stay in touch, calling and e-mailing, and you probably do for a while. But it is hard to maintain a close friendship with someone you can't see. You are sharing different experiences and you know different people so you have less and less in common. It really helps your friendship if you can SEE each other.

How does that thought translate into your relationship with God? You can't really SEE God. You can't HEAR His voice on the phone. Much of being God's friend has to be taken by faith. You trust Him because of what you read about Him in the Bible and what others teach you about Him. You trust Him because of a history with Him and the promise of a future with Him.

ChallengePoint

Trust in God is founded on faith – believing in what you cannot actually see. The reward for that is glorious, inexpressible joy!

Knowing God by
Using His Gifts

"Here I am! I stand at the door and knock. If you hear My voice and open the door, I will come in and eat with you, and you will eat with Me."

＊ REVELATION 3:20

There is a famous old painting about this Scripture verse. It shows Jesus standing at a wooden door, knocking on it. The interesting thing is that the door does not have a handle on the outside. Jesus can't go in until the door is opened – from the inside.

What does this have to do with using God's gifts? The gift is Jesus. God gives you a chance to have a friendship with Him … to sit down and chat with Him. But you have to open the door to let Him in.

ChallengePoint

What a gift – Jesus will share a meal with you. Even more amazing is that Jesus knocks at the door of your heart and waits for you to open it. He doesn't come barreling in like a bull in a china shop. He waits for you to invite Him in.

Knowing God by
His Love

When the kindness and love of God our Savior appeared, He saved us, not because of righteous things we had done, but because of His mercy. He saved us through the washing of rebirth and renewal by the Holy Spirit.

✻ TITUS 3:4-5

Ugh, don't you get tired of girls who act so interested in you with their syrupy sweet comments and questions, but their actions show they don't care a bit about you? They don't sit beside you at lunch or invite you to their homes … actions speak louder than words.

You've probably heard that statement before and the fact is – it's really true. You can SAY whatever you think you're supposed to say, but if your actions don't back it up; people will pay more attention to your actions and will think your words are just false. Here's the cool thing about God – He doesn't just talk about loving you, His actions back up His words. He saves you from your sins – love can't get any more active than that.

ChallengePoint

OK, you know God loves you because His actions show it. God's actions wash away your sins and give you new life through the Holy Spirit – also a gift from Him. Words of love backed up by actions of love.

Praying

And this is the boldness we have in God's presence: that if we ask God for anything that agrees with what He wants, He hears us.

✳ 1 JOHN 5:14

Kids are sometimes accused of having selective hearing. This means that you might not hear your mom ask you to do something (that you don't really want to do). But a friend could whisper something from down the street, with music blaring, and you have earmuffs on … and somehow you hear her! OK, maybe that's exaggerating a little, but the point is, you hear what you want to hear.

Does God have selective hearing? Kind of. He does hear your prayers – all of them. When you ask God for help, He hears you on the first try. He promises that. But the key to productive prayers is asking for things that are in His will. What's that all about? Well, if you ask Him to make an enemy crash and burn – He probably won't pay much attention – but if you ask for things that show love for Him and others, He will hear right away.

ChallengePoint

God wants to hear your prayers. He wants to answer them too. The prayers of someone who is trying to obey God and live for Him will please God.

Seeking His Protection

Then you will experience God's peace, which exceeds anything we can understand. His peace will guard your hearts and minds as you live in Christ Jesus.

* PHILIPPIANS 4:7

Picture this image: a rocky cliff hanging over an ocean. Waves crashing against the cliff as the wind fiercely blows. Nothing can stay on those rocks; the waves and wind wash everything away. Except … you notice in one tiny little crack in the cliff a small yellow flower pushing up. It's protected from the wind and the waves around it. It's growing in a place of peace.

That's an image of God's peace. Things may be crashing and blowing around you – worry, fear, self-centeredness and low self-esteem crash against your heart day after day. But God's peace is the protection that cushions your heart so it is not broken by the wind or waves.

ChallengePoint

God's peace protects your heart and mind. You need that protection from Him to live in peace and obedience to Him.

Knowing God by
Serving Him

Jesus said to His followers, "If people want to follow Me, they must give up the things they want. They must be willing even to give up their lives to follow Me."

* MATTHEW 16:24

Deny yourself? Wow, that's pretty hard, isn't it? The message of this verse is "Get yourself out of the way." Plain and simple. You can't serve God and keep your own agenda going of how everything is about you. Know why? IT ISN'T ABOUT YOU.

Forget promoting yourself. Forget worrying about how everything affects you. Just follow God. Do what God wants you to do – even the stuff that isn't so much fun. Just follow Him.

ChallengePoint

Getting yourself out of the way is not easy. It means focusing on God and what He wants first, then focusing on other people next. You come last. Some of the stuff God wants you to do may be stuff you don't enjoy. It may be background stuff that pushes someone else to star status. It may be dirty work. So what? It's what God wants you to do, and serving God is about Him, not you.

Knowing God by
Obeying Him

So you have not received a spirit that makes you fearful slaves. Instead, you received God's Spirit when He adopted you as His own children. Now we call Him, "Abba, Father."

* ROMANS 8:15

Honesty time: Are you friends with someone who insists that you always do what she says? Does it seem as though she doesn't even think you have a brain? Wow, that's no fun. It's like you are her slave. A slave just does what she is told to do. She does not think for herself. Often her obedience is based on fear; in your case, perhaps you are scared that your "friend" won't be your friend anymore.

Obeying God is not like that. God adopted you as His child. You are family because He's your Father. Hopefully you know that means that you don't need to fear Him. You obey Him because you love Him and He loves you.

ChallengePoint

It may be hard to imagine what a slave's life is like. Hopefully you will never have to know. As God's child you have His Holy Spirit living in you. You are His child. The desire to obey Him should then come from love for Him.

Knowing God by
Being Like Christ

Keep your lives free from the love of money, and be satisfied with what you have. God has said, "I will never leave you; I will never abandon you."

* HEBREWS 13:5

As far as most of the world is concerned, the biggest sign of success is: Money! Money! Money! Get more money! Make more money! It's all about MONEY! That's the message that television, movies, Internet and magazines throw at you every day.

Most of the world thinks that success is only indicated by how much money you make. However, God says that's not true. He says it is more important to be satisfied with what you have – your wealth comes from the fact that God will always help you. He will always be with you. Money will not. You can't take it to heaven with you.

ChallengePoint

Of course, you need money to live. But don't make grabbing lots of money your focus in life. When Jesus lived on earth, He didn't even have a home. He depended on others for a place to sleep and for food to eat. He was satisfied with that. It goes against everything the world teaches, but the truth is, real wealth comes from having God in your life.

Knowing God by
His Forgiveness

Since God chose you to be the holy people He loves, you must clothe yourselves with tenderhearted mercy, kindness, humility, gentleness, and patience. Make allowance for each other's faults, and forgive anyone who offends you. Remember, the Lord forgave you, so you must forgive others.

✳ COLOSSIANS 3:12-13

Do you like to shop? It's fun to try on clothes, wander from store to store and look at different styles. It's really fun to shop with your mom or a friend and get another opinion on how an outfit looks on you. Do you have a "look"? That means you have a style that most of your clothes reflect. It's what you're comfortable in.

Are you comfortable in the "clothes" that you should be wearing as a member of God's family? He chose to make you holy like He is and that means you should exhibit the same qualities He has – kindness, gentleness, patience and forgiveness.

ChallengePoint

Put on the clothes that God gives you when He makes you a member of His family. One of the major parts of that outfit is forgiveness. Others should be able to see God in how you live and act. He forgives you every day … pass that along to others.

Knowing God by
Understanding Anger

"But I promise you that if you are angry with someone, you will have to stand trial. If you call someone a fool, you will be taken to court. And if you say that someone is worthless, you will be in danger of the fires of hell."

∗ MATTHEW 5:22

Anger is usually self-centered. Anger never gets you your way. Anger only hurts relationships. Anger does not please God. God is SERIOUS about anger, so you'd better keep yours under control. Look at this:

1. Get angry – you're going to be judged for it.
2. Call someone names – you could be taken to court.
3. Curse someone – you're in danger of the fires of hell.

God doesn't mess around with anger.

ChallengePoint

Nothing good ever comes from anger. Pay attention to this verse when you get mad at someone. STOP and ask God to help you keep your emotions under control! Anger hurts others. Anger doesn't show God's love to others.

Put on your new nature, created to be like God – truly righteous and holy.

* EPHESIANS 4:24

God gives you a new nature when He saves you. What does that mean? Well, before you were saved, you were, to put it simply, dirty. You're dirty because your heart is self-centered, not God-centered. That shows in selfishness, anger, greed … ugly things. You are stained by sin.

When God saves you, He gives you a clean, new nature. A nature that is God-centered and love-focused. You get to start over and be like God, righteous and holy.

ChallengePoint

You know God loves you because He cleans up your dirty heart. He gives you a clean new heart that wants to serve Him and obey Him. Of course, this isn't a new physical heart that pumps blood in your body – it's the heart in your spirit and soul that wants to serve Him. He makes you clean and new!

Knowing God by
Being Thankful

He threw himself at Jesus' feet and thanked Him – and he was a Samaritan.

* LUKE 17:16

Do you know what's interesting about this Scripture verse? It's from a story about ten guys who had a terrible disease. They had a disease that was so bad they couldn't live in town near other people. They even had to leave their families. Jesus healed all ten men. All ten men were so excited to be healed that they ran to town without even saying thanks.

But one man came back when he remembered that he hadn't thanked Jesus. This one man was a Samaritan – an enemy of the Jews, Jesus' people. Weird, huh?

ChallengePoint

A man who in any other circumstance would have been Jesus' enemy, fell at His feet and thanked Him for His healing power. Nine men who were of the same nationality and faith as Jesus did not take time to say thanks. Learn from this Samaritan man ... thank Jesus for all He does for you.

Knowing God by
Celebrating Him

So at the name of Jesus everyone will bow down, those in heaven, on earth, and under the earth.

✳ PHILIPPIANS 2:10

Do your parents ever suggest the Quiet Game when your family is on car trips? Of course, it's a trick to make you and the other kids quiet down a little when you're excited about going on vacation. But it makes you wonder if a celebration can be quiet. Does a celebration have to mean giggling, shouting and dancing with your friends?

Can a celebration be quiet and awestruck? It would appear so. One day every person will drop to their knees in worship at the very name of Jesus. It's hard to shout and cheer when you're kneeling. This is serious, though, because for some people it will be too late – they will be recognizing Jesus from the condemned place of hell. They need to hear about His love now!

ChallengePoint

Celebrate Him. Worship Him. Tell others about Him. Bow your knees before Him and confess Him with your voice.

Being Like Christ

You are not controlled by your sinful nature. You are controlled by the Spirit if you have the Spirit of God living in you. (And remember that those who do not have the Spirit of Christ living in them do not belong to Him at all.)

* ROMANS 8:9

Marionette puppets are controlled by strings. The puppeteer stands above them with strings in her hand that move the puppets' arms and legs. The puppeteer decides where the puppet goes and how it acts. Control is the issue – who controls you?

If the Holy Spirit is living in you because you've asked Christ into your heart, then He is the One in control of you … not your old sinful nature.

ChallengePoint

The problem is that your old sinful nature never really goes away. It keeps trying to get the strings controlling your heart back in its hands. It's a constant battle, and one that you help the Holy Spirit win by daily giving your life to Him. Make the choice to put the control in His hands.

Knowing God by
Being Like Christ

We all make many mistakes. If people never said anything wrong, they would be perfect and able to control their entire selves, too.

✳ JAMES 3:2

Sometimes words slide out of your mouth that you wish you could pull back in, right? Everyone has experiences of speaking without thinking, and nothing good comes from that. Controlling what you say and how you say it is so very hard! And, unfortunately, the words you say often hurt other people and even damage your reputation as a Christ-follower.

Of course, if you could control your words then you could control your thoughts and actions too. The bottom line is that it is not going to happen, so you'd better ask God for His help.

ChallengePoint

The only way to have any success controlling your words, thoughts or actions is by asking the help of the Holy Spirit. Ask Him to help you control your words, thoughts and actions. Ask Him to help you live like Christ.

Knowing God by
Loving Others

Jesus answered, "The most important command is this: 'Listen, people of Israel! The Lord our God is the only Lord. Love the Lord your God with all your heart, all your soul, all your mind, and all your strength.' The second command is this: 'Love your neighbor as you love yourself.' There are no commands more important than these."

＊ MARK 12:29-31

Love, love, love. It is the theme of God's message to the world. Love God most of all – MOST OF ALL. Then, love others as much as you love yourself.

Why does this theme keep showing up? Because it's important. God insists on your complete devotion, heart, soul, mind and strength. There are some things in life that you can get away with giving only half your attention to … loving God is not one of them.

ChallengePoint

Attention to loving God and loving others needs to be complete. An unwillingness to fully commit to loving God is unacceptable. Don't ride the fence on this. Give God everything. You'll never be sorry.

Knowing God by
Showing Love

Most important of all, continue to show deep love for each other, for love covers a multitude of sins.

* 1 Peter 4:8

This verse explains love being like a blanket. How? Well, you live with other people. You go to school with other people. You are around people all the time. There will undoubtedly be times when you don't get things right – times when you mess up and do dumb things like say mean things, be selfish, criticize, gossip … get it?

That's when the love blanket comes in. It covers over those things. People will forgive you for your bad behavior if they know that you really do love them. Your love for them comes from God's love for you.

ChallengePoint

Love is necessary in relating to others. It's important because God says it's important. You know that if someone says something mean to you but you know that deep down inside they really love you, then you're much more likely to forgive them. Let your love for others show.

And after you suffer for a short time, God will make everything right. He will make you strong and support you and keep you from falling. He called you to share in His glory in Christ, a glory that will continue forever.

> * 1 PETER 5:9-10

Why do bad things happen to good people? Because this world is full of sin – has been ever since Adam and Eve tasted that fruit. Sin causes people to do mean things to each other. Sin is what allowed sickness and death to enter life. So, life is stinky sometimes. There's no way around that. Bad things happen, even to good people.

When the bad things come, do you wonder where God is? Do you wonder why He doesn't just fix things for you? That question has been asked a million times over the years. There is no easy answer. But one reason is that it is when things get tough and you need help that you see God's power. You experience Him helping you, lifting you up and strengthening you.

ChallengePoint

The message is "Keep on keeping on." Keep trusting God. Problems are necessary in order to appreciate good times. The stress of problems makes your faith grow stronger. Trust God enough to endure the tough times.

"Teach these new disciples to obey all the commands I have given you. And be sure of this: I am with you always, even to the end of the age."

* Matthew 28:20

Two gifts from God are outlined here:

1. People who will teach you about God's commands. How awesome is that? You don't have to figure things out on your own. God provides help.
2. God will always be with you – forever. Well, it doesn't get any better than that.

It's pretty cool how God instructs people to help each other learn about Him. Then He encourages you to keep on doing His work with His strength and presence which will always be with you.

ChallengePoint

Thank God for His gifts which help you live life for Him. Thank Him that you never have to do this alone – God is always with you!

Knowing God by
Loving Others

We love because God loved us first.

✳ 1 JOHN 4:19

Do you take piano lessons (or any other instrument)? If you want to improve your skills on your instrument a good teacher is very important. The best way to learn something is from someone who has already mastered the skill.

Learn from the master, right? Well, you can sure do that when it comes to learning how to love. God loved you first – before time began; in fact, before YOU began. He loves you no matter what. He is the Master in knowing how to love so He can sure teach you how to do it.

ChallengePoint

God commands you to love others. But He doesn't leave you on your own to figure out how to do it. God loved you first. As you experience God's love, which is completely undeserved, you should be more willing to love others. If you can't or don't know how, let God teach you.

Knowing God by
Seeking His Guidance

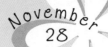

Your commands make me wiser than my enemies, because they are mine forever.

* PSALM 119:98

Have you ever played one of those trivia games where you compete with other players to answer questions from different categories? History, music, science … the person who has the most information usually wins the game. That's true in life too.

Having God's Word to guide you and teach you gives you all the information you need to live in obedience to Him. His Word shows you what is right and wrong. His Word should be your constant guide. It is your advantage in this life – it makes you smarter than your enemies.

ChallengePoint

God's Word is only your guidebook if you use it. So, spend time each day reading His Word. Look for His guidance in His words, look for instructions as to how you should live for Him.

Knowing God by
Serving Him

Do not be fooled: You cannot cheat God. People harvest only what they plant.

* GALATIANS 6:7

If you keep on doing what you do, you'll keep on getting what you got. OK, not good grammar, but the message is there. What you put into life determines what you get out of it.

How does that witty little phrase relate to serving God? Like this: What you put into serving God is what you get out of it. If you continually do things in a half-hearted way, not growing or improving in your walk with God, don't expect major joy and blessings.

ChallengePoint

The gardening example in this verse is that you will harvest what you plant. That's fair. It puts responsibility on you to make a choice as to how you will live your life. Are you going to give God everything? If you're not, then don't expect Him to give you everything.

Knowing God by
Obeying Him

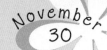

The LORD leads with unfailing love and faithfulness all who keep His covenant and obey His demands.

✳ PSALM 25:10

Training to run a race takes hours of hard work, every day. It takes paying attention to your schedule, your diet and your body. It's work. The reward is when you step onto the track and know that you are ready to run because you have trained to the best of your ability.

Obeying God has rewards too. It's not always easy and it is a learning process, but the reward is God's unfailing love and faithfulness to you. What could be better than that?

ChallengePoint

The joy of having God lead you and knowing that His love is constant is worth the effort of obeying God. You do not have to learn to obey by yourself, God will help you. His Word will teach and guide you.

A laugh is a smile that bursts.
~ MARY H. WALDRIP

December

Knowing God by
Serving Him

You yourself must be an example to them by doing good works of every kind. Let everything you do reflect the integrity and seriousness of your teaching.

* TITUS 2:7

Anyone can be an ambassador. In fact, pretty much everyone is an ambassador of their own beliefs and of the things they care the most about. You might be an ambassador for your love of horseback riding, ice skating, a music group you love … you get the idea.

An ambassador sings the praises of whatever she's representing or passionate about – she's almost like a cheerleader who tries to influence others to join her in her passion. Regardless of what else you represent, you are already an ambassador – of God. That means you need to be careful how you live, what you say and how you represent God.

ChallengePoint

Did you know that everything you do reflects what you really feel about God? Yeah, it does. If you are kind, loving and respectful, that shows that you take God's teaching seriously. If you aren't … well, then it appears that He doesn't mean much to you. It takes an effort to think about how you live, what you say and how you represent God. But it's important.

Knowing God by
Obeying Him

"If you obey My commands, you will remain in My love, just as I have obeyed My Father's commands and remain in His love."

* JOHN 15:10

Examples help, right? Say you're trying to learn a new math skill, it helps to have examples in the book of how to solve the problems. If you're trying a new recipe, it helps to have pictures of what it should look like when you're finished. Examples always help.

Jesus gave you an example to follow. His example of obedience to God's laws was constant and steady. Obeying God keeps your relationship with Him healthy. Your communication with Him, your understanding and experience of His love … all is well.

ChallengePoint

Thank God for the example of how Jesus lived. It really helps to know that He experienced the same temptations you do and still He chose to obey God. Obeying God's commandments keeps your relationship with Him healthy. So you never need to doubt His love for you. Jesus is your model.

Knowing God by
His Forgiveness

You were cleansed; you were made holy; you were made right with God by calling on the name of the Lord Jesus Christ and by the Spirit of our God.

✳ 1 CORINTHIANS 6:11

Do you like to bake cookies? When you bake cookies, you have a recipe to follow and some things have to be done in order. You can't bake the cookies until the dough is mixed. You can't finish the dough without all the ingredients. It's a process.

Look at the process in which God's forgiveness builds as it is outlined in this verse. First you are cleaned up (your sins are washed away). Then you are made holy (set apart for God's work), and then you are made right with God by Jesus' name (a relationship is begun that will grow stronger and stronger over time). God's forgiveness of your sin opens the doorway to this process.

ChallengePoint

It's a simple process because God wants it to be. He wants salvation to be available to anyone who wants it because He loves all people. God's forgiveness is available to anyone who asks for it.

Knowing God by
Seeking His Guidance

God always does what He plans, and that's why He appointed Christ to choose us.

✳ EPHESIANS 1:11

Your friend invites you to go to a movie that you've both been very excited about seeing. You look forward to it, anticipating how great it will be and how much fun the two of you will have talking about it afterward. But when you get to the theater, she insists on going to see a different movie … one you've already seen! Wow, that's frustrating, disappointing, confusing and, well, it stinks.

Fickle is the word to describe your friend right now. It means she can't make a decision and stick with it. You never have to worry about God being fickle. He has a plan for your life and He sticks with it. He doesn't change His mind half way through. You can count on it.

ChallengePoint

OK, it may seem at times that God has changed His mind about something. But, He doesn't. He knows what He's doing but He has to take you through a process sometimes so that you can learn certain lessons. Trust His guidance, whatever it is. You'll be glad you did.

Knowing God by
His Faithfulness

"However, those the Father has given Me will come to Me, and I will never reject them."

✳ JOHN 6:37

There is an old saying that the only things you can count on are death and taxes. Yeah, everyone dies eventually – and taxes … well, you don't really have to worry about that yet. But, what can you absolutely count on in this world? That everyone will die? Yes, except when they don't (there are a couple of guys in the Bible who got to go to heaven without dying first); that the sun will always come up in the morning and set at night? Yes, except when it doesn't (it happened once in the Old Testament). That the oceans will stay put where they're supposed to be? Yes, except when they don't (remember the Red Sea?).

There is only one thing you can absolutely count on and that is God. When you come to the Father, you become His and He will always, always be with you.

✳ ChallengePoint

It's wonderful to know that God means what He says and that He never changes His mind. You can count on this forever, no matter what. God says that once you are His, He will never reject you. Never.

Knowing God by
Seeking His Protection

The Lord is faithful, and He will strengthen and protect you from the evil one.

✳ 2 THESSALONIANS 3:3

Don't ever doubt that there is an evil presence in this world. It's easy to forget about Satan when things are going well and you're busy with your friends. You spend time laughing and talking and you can forget that he is always hard at work.

Of course, you can't blame everything on him, but some of the rotten things in this world are certainly because of him. It's wonderful to know that God is standing guard over you. He protects you from the Evil One.

ChallengePoint

The only way to enjoy God's protection is to stay close to Him. He will take care of you. There is an evil presence in the world that is constantly trying to trip you up and make you fall away from God. Only God can protect you.

Let the word of Christ dwell in you richly as you teach and admonish one another with all wisdom, and as you sing psalms, hymns and spiritual songs with gratitude in your hearts to God.

✳ COLOSSIANS 3:16

Words. How many words do you think you speak in a day? How many words do you hear? How many words do you read? Words are input to your heart. The words you hear and even the words you think are putting ideas and opinions in your heart.

Are you putting healthy things in your heart? Things that honor God? Things that will fill your heart with thankfulness for who God is and all He does for you? Be careful what you put in your heart – it makes a difference.

ChallengePoint

Good stuff that comes from Christ's words going into your heart includes wisdom and thankfulness. Good things come from the words of Christ in your life. His words give you a lot to be thankful for.

Knowing God by
Celebrating Him

This will happen on that day when the Lord returns to be praised and honored by all who have faith in Him and belong to Him. This includes you, because you believed what we said.

 * 2 THESSALONIANS 1:10

What is the biggest celebration you've ever seen? It might have been on the TV, but things as major as the opening of the Olympics or a celebration by a candidate who wins an election are pretty big examples. Or a city's celebration when their professional team wins a big championship. There's usually a big parade with people lining the streets cheering for the team. Quite a celebration!

Well, there's going to be a celebration like that for Jesus when He comes back to earth. Everyone on earth will recognize Him as the Lord – the Son of God. It will be the most awesome celebration ever!

ChallengePoint

The day will come when the whole earth recognizes God's power and His place as Creator and Savior. The celebration will be like nothing you've ever experienced. What an exciting thing to look forward to!

Knowing God by
Being Like Christ

"And you will know the truth, and the truth will set you free."
* JOHN 8:32

Have you ever played the game Telephone? A group of people sit in a circle. One person whispers a statement to the person next to her, who passes it on to the person beside her, who passes it on … until it has gone around the entire circle. By the time the statement is said aloud at the end, it barely resembles what the original statement was. The "truth" of the first statement is completely gone.

What is truth anyway? The only absolute-for-sure truth comes from the Bible. Do you memorize Bible verses? Why should you? Because those Scripture verses are the key to surviving problems you face and even to growing stronger in your faith. Jesus quoted Scripture back to Satan when He was being tempted by Satan. If it was important for Jesus to know Scripture, then it must be important for you too.

ChallengePoint

Memorizing verses is important because then they are embedded in your mind. Jesus often quoted Scripture. That means He must have read the Old Testament and committed it to memory. The verses of the Bible are the weapons you need to fight against Satan's attacks.

Knowing God by
Being Like Christ

You are joined together with peace through the Spirit, so make every effort to continue together in this way.

✳ EPHESIANS 4:3

In the game Red Rover a team of kids join hands and stand in a line. They hold tightly to each other as a player from the opposing team tries to break through. Those team members are united. They are holding tightly to each other.

Being united with your teammates is absolutely necessary. You are on Christ's team with other Christians. It's really important for Christians to be united in the Holy Spirit. That unity keeps you at peace with others.

ChallengePoint

Is it hard to get along with everyone all the time? Sure it is, but God's children need to live at peace with one another. Other people are watching to see how you behave. They notice whether or not you get along with each other and love each other.

Knowing God by
Being Like Christ

Do everything without complaining and arguing, so that no one can criticize you. Live clean, innocent lives as children of God, shining like bright lights in a world full of crooked and perverse people.

✳ PHILIPPIANS 2:14-15

Jesus said that His followers are like bright lights on a dark hillside. You know what that's like. Go outside on a dark night and look up. What do you see? The white lights of stars shining brightly in the darkness. Anyone can see those lights, and you can be sure that people are watching you.

Who is watching? Everyone who knows that you claim to be a Christ-follower. Yep, so every time you gripe about something or argue with someone, they notice that. Your job in living like Christ is to be a good representative of Him. Shine brightly – look different than people who don't know Him.

ChallengePoint

Christ trusts you to live a life that shows what He is like. Get along with other people. Don't be selfish or self-centered. Live a life that shows His love to those around you.

Knowing God by
Showing Love

Anyone who claims to be in the light but hates his brother is still in the darkness.

* 1 JOHN 2:9

So, you know the right "Christian" things to say. You've gone to church your whole life and you know how to "sound" Christian. You may be able to quote Bible verses and pray beautiful prayers, but that doesn't mean you are following Christ.

There is one evidence of living for Christ that is hard to fake – loving others. Loving those who are not very nice. Loving those who are different from you. Loving those you don't really like. Yeah. Those. You can claim to be a God-follower and maybe convince people around you since you can say all the right things. But you won't convince God that it's the truth if you don't back up your words with loving the people around you.

ChallengePoint

It is very important to God that you love others. He says it over and over. It is actually a family likeness. So, if you're really a part of God's family, that love will be there.

Knowing God by
Showing Courage

Obey the LORD with great fear. Be happy, but tremble.

* PSALM 2:11

Serving God is such a privilege. Why does this verse attach fear to it? Well, sometimes it is scary because of the responsibility of being God's co-worker. You don't want to mess up God's work or represent Him badly to those around you.

So, you need courage to be God's servant. Courage to do the job He gives you. Courage to do it well. Courage to be steady and constant in your service. Then, courage to rejoice in the privilege of serving.

ChallengePoint

When you go ahead and do what God wants, even though it's scary to you, it shows you trust Him to take care of you and keep on guiding you. That's something to celebrate!

"Heal the sick, raise the dead to life again, heal those who have skin diseases, and force demons out of people. I give you these powers freely, so help other people freely."

* MATTHEW 10:8

There aren't many times in life when you get something for nothing. If you do get something for free, it may not be something you would actually be happy to have. However, on the opposite side of the spectrum, everything you've gotten from God, you got for free. You paid nothing for it and it is all amazing. For example, God's forgiveness, His love and the incredible gift of salvation are all things you received without paying.

Now, God wants you to give without expecting payment in return. God wants you to give and give and give out of whatever He has given you. Maybe all you can give is time or prayers. That's OK. Give what you can.

ChallengePoint

It's really important to give to others because it ties you together. It makes you a part of the same family. Helping others is the best feeling in the world. Give as often as you can in any way you can.

Seeking His Protection

"Take My yoke upon you. Let Me teach you, because I am humble and gentle at heart, and you will find rest for your souls."

✻ MATTHEW 11:29

Are you a "joiner"? Do you join as many clubs and teams as you can? This Scripture verse is an invitation to join with Jesus. The simple explanation of this Scripture verse is that Jesus is encouraging you to identify with Him – join His team – line up with Him.

When you do that, He will teach you about living for Him and loving God. He will teach you about gentleness and humility – something He is an expert on.

ChallengePoint

When you join Jesus' family, you can take a deep breath and relax. You can rest because He will take care of you, protect you and teach you.

But the Spirit produces the fruit of love, joy, peace, patience, kindness, goodness, faithfulness, gentleness, self-control. There is no law that says these things are wrong.

✳ GALATIANS 5:22-23

Know what's interesting about this Scripture verse? All nine of the characteristics listed here as fruit of the Spirit are one fruit. See, it says fruit, not fruits. One fruit with nine different qualities.

So, when the Holy Spirit lives in you all of these qualities should show in the way you treat other people and the way you live. The Holy Spirit works in your heart to teach you these characteristics. You don't have to learn them on your own.

ChallengePoint

The Holy Spirit put those nine things in your heart. He planted them there and He will help you learn how to let them shine out in your life.

Seeking His Guidance

David shepherded them with integrity of heart; with skillful hands he led them.

* PSALM 78:72

Any time you visit a foreign country it helps to have a guide. A guide who speaks the language and knows his way around the city makes the trip much more enjoyable. Otherwise you waste a lot of time just trying to figure things out.

David was called "a man after God's own heart." He sought God's wisdom and guidance and then passed it along to others. God wants to be your guide. He's already been where you are going – deeper into a life of obedience and living for Him.

ChallengePoint

The Christian life is much easier with a guide, and the best one to have is God Himself. Why does God want to be your guide? Because He loves you. He cares about you so He will guide you in living for Him.

Being Obedient

"I correct and discipline everyone I love. So be diligent and turn from your indifference."

* REVELATION 3:19

How do your parents discipline you? Are you grounded or do you have privileges taken away? Whatever method is used … it's no fun. As your Father, God disciplines you. He has to because that's how you learn from your disobedience.

Don't be discouraged when God disciplines you, be glad that He cares enough to do that. Learn from it and try harder to be obedient the next time.

ChallengePoint

It is frustrating to your parents when you continually disobey in the same area. It's got to be frustrating to God, too, because it means you aren't learning from your mistakes. Or it could mean that you just don't care enough to pay attention. That's sad. Pay attention and learn what you can so that you will be more and more obedient.

Knowing God by
Seeking His Protection

The LORD will not abandon His people.

* 1 SAMUEL 12:22

Sometimes you hear on the news of a newborn baby who has been abandoned by its mother. The woman has the baby but then just leaves it in a garbage can or under a bush and she runs away. She doesn't even wait around to see if someone rescues the child. So sad.

That is NOT what God will do. He promises to stick with you when you have hard times in your life. He will never run away from you. He will not get tired of your problems and He will never be overwhelmed by your problems. He loves you and He will keep on helping as much as He can.

ChallengePoint

It's so cool to know that you are never alone. You will never get in the middle of a problem, look around, and find that God has bailed out on you. God promises to be with you, help you and guide you.

Thank God for His gift that is too wonderful for words!

✳ 2 CORINTHIANS 9:15

Do you write thank-you notes for birthday or Christmas gifts? Good for your mom if she taught you to do that. It's kind of hard, though, to be thankful for gifts like … a super ugly sweater. It's hard to say much about stuff that you may need but don't really want.

God gave you an amazing gift – too wonderful for words. He thought of a gift that you not only NEED but that you would WANT. Jesus. Have you thanked Him for this amazing gift?

ChallengePoint

Jesus changes everything about your life. Jesus makes salvation possible and being with God forever possible. He makes living everyday life better and your relationships with others better. Good gift, huh? Remember to thank Him.

Knowing God by
Suppressing Our Pride

We are not saying that we can do this work ourselves. It is God who makes us able to do all that we do.

✳ 2 CORINTHIANS 3:5

God covers this topic a lot in the Bible. He is not a fan of pride. Tooting your own horn gets you nowhere with Him. There is nothing you brag about that you can take credit for.

Seriously, bragging about yourself and your accomplishments would be like a tree bragging about growing leaves. Who made those leaves grow? God. Who put the branches on the tree? God. Who grew the tree itself? God. Get it?

ChallengePoint

There is no reason at all to brag. You can't take credit for all the things that you can do. Your skills, abilities, talents and intelligence all come from God. You can claim no credit for it. However, you can ... and should ... thank Him every day!

Knowing God by
Serving Him

And Solomon, my son, learn to know the God of your ancestors intimately. Worship and serve Him with your whole heart and a willing mind. For the LORD sees every heart and knows every plan and thought. If you seek Him, you will find Him. But if you forsake Him, He will reject you forever.

* 1 CHRONICLES 28:9

The intimacy this Scripture verse suggests is startling. First, get to know God intimately. That means get to know Him very, very well. The only way that will happen is to spend a lot of time with Him so you know the way He thinks and the way He acts.

Once you know Him well, worship and serve Him with your whole heart … willingly, because you can't fake it with God. He sees your heart and mind so he knows what your motivation is. Seek Him – look for Him all the time and you will find Him.

ChallengePoint

If you want to serve God, give it all you have. Get to know Him. Talk with Him. Read His Word. Make sure your heart is devoted to Him because that's what He looks at – not all the stuff you are doing – but WHY you are doing it.

"When you cross deep rivers, I will be with you, and you won't drown. When you walk through fire, you won't be burned or scorched by the flames."

✳ ISAIAH 43:2

When you climb in a boat, do you look around to see if there are life jackets? It's good to know where they are just in case there is some problem. A life jacket is one of those things that you hope you never need, but if you do, you're so glad for it. It will keep you from going under if you happen to fall into the water.

Unfortunately, you will have trouble in your life. Life just gets stinky sometimes and you have to deal with it. BUT you don't have to deal with it alone. God promises to stick close to you and hold you up, just like a life jacket. He promises to be with you in all those stinky times. You'll never be alone.

ChallengePoint

Isn't it nice to know that you don't have to face the hard times alone? God is with you and that means He is strengthening you, helping you and guiding you. You don't have to plough through problems by yourself.

Knowing God by
His Love

"Even to your old age and gray hairs I am He, I am He who will sustain you. I have made you and I will carry you; I will sustain you and I will rescue you."

✳ Isaiah 46:4

Love never gives up. It just keeps giving and giving. God's love for you began with His plan to send Jesus to earth as a baby. It continued throughout Jesus' lifetime as He taught about God. Then it shined brightest when Jesus died for your sins and was raised back to life.

God's love lasts forever. He promises to stick close beside you throughout your whole life, even to your old age, strengthening you and encouraging you. He will protect you and guide you … forever.

ChallengePoint

God's love is what sent Jesus to earth on that first Christmas long ago. It was the beginning of His plan to make a way for you to be able to know Him. He promises to take care of you for your whole life. His love holds you close so you're never alone!

Knowing God by
Obeying Him

"This is the new covenant I will make with the people of Israel on that day," says the Lord: "I will put My laws in their minds, and I will write them on their hearts. I will be their God, and they will be My people."

* HEBREWS 8:10

The first day of school your teacher assigns a big project that will involve lots of research, creativity and writing. Then you will make a presentation to the class. This job is big, but it's a little easier because the teacher gives you an outline of what is expected. That helps. You don't have to figure things out by yourself.

God has promised that if you choose to obey Him, He will tell you exactly what is expected. He loves you and wants you to be successful in obeying Him, so He will help you know His laws by putting them in your mind and heart. It's easier to obey them when you know what they are.

ChallengePoint

Obeying God is not always easy because Satan will do everything he can to stop you. Temptation and confusion are a couple of his specialties. But God will help you remember His laws because He wants you to succeed. You're not in this alone. Cool, huh?

Knowing God by
Seeking His Protection

God is strong and can help you not to fall. He can bring you before His glory without any wrong in you and can give you great joy. He is the only God, the One who saves us. To Him be glory, greatness, power, and authority through Jesus Christ our Lord for all time past, now, and forever.

* JUDE 1:24-25

Are these Scripture verses saying that you will never fall down? You'll never trip while you're running or catch your toe on a stone and fall down? No, this is actually talking about stumbling in your Christian walk. God will keep you from falling so far away from Him that you can't find your way back. Of course, you need to ask for this kind of protection.

Stay close to God so that He can protect you by cushioning your falls – yes, you'll still stumble sometimes, He doesn't stop that – but He doesn't let the fall seriously hurt your relationship with Him. He wants you to learn from your stumbles, but not to give up because of them.

ChallengePoint

Wow! God loves you a lot! Just think about Him grabbing you when it seems like you're going to fall on your face and then setting you back on your feet. He will protect you all the way into His presence in heaven.

Being Like Christ

Then God said, "Let Us make human beings in Our image, to be like Us."

✳ GENESIS 1:26

Wow. God's creation of the first man is amazing to think about. Seriously, God took a pile of dirt and made it into the first man by breathing life into him. That's amazing and a gigantic miracle. Then He took a rib out of that first man and made the first woman. Amazing again.

But even more amazing is that the first man and woman were made in God's image. They could do things God could do – think, feel, love, make decisions. And you are like those first people. Made in God's image.

ChallengePoint

God planned it that the people He created would be like Him. That's why people partner with Him in His work on this planet. You are like God and that means you are like Christ. It also means you have a job to do! Quite a responsibility, eh?

Knowing God by
Giving

"Do to others whatever you would like them to do to you."

✳ MATTHEW 7:12

What would you like people to do for you? How would you like them to treat you? Why don't you treat them that way first? If you treat others with kindness you are more likely to get kindness back from them. If you treat them with sarcasm and rudeness, guess what? You're likely to get that same thing back from them.

God's wish, of course, is that you will show love and kindness to others and will share what He has given you with all you meet. Remember, His focus is loving others all the time.

ChallengePoint

This verse is often called The Golden Rule. It's a foundational statement for how to treat others. But don't just be kind only so others will be kind back. That's a good starting point, but make every effort to be kind so that others will be able to see what God is like by how you live your life.

Trusting Him

In times of trouble, God is with us, and when we are knocked down, we get up again.

* 2 CORINTHIANS 4:9

There's a child's toy that is a plastic doll filled with air. It has a weighted bottom, so when you punch it, it falls backwards or to the side, but then it comes right back up to a standing position.

Sometimes when problems keep smacking you in the face, it's tempting to just fall down and stay down. Maybe you think the problems will stop if you stay down. But you don't stay down, because you know God is there helping you. He helps you bounce back up just like that child's toy, brushes the dust off your back and helps you keep on going.

ChallengePoint

You can trust God to help you every time you need help. He is always there. Sometimes you can't sense His presence until you actually need His help. Then, BOOM, there He is!

Jesus wept.

✶ JOHN 11:35

Some girls cry all the time – when they are happy, when they are sad or when they are confused. They just cry. But usually a person doesn't cry over something she doesn't care about.

There are a couple of times recorded in the Bible when Jesus cried. Does that amaze you? If He didn't care He wouldn't cry. Here's the formula:

Jesus loves.
He sees people hurting.
He cries.

ChallengePoint

It's amazing to think about God feeling pain or sadness because of you, isn't it? But He loves you and when you love someone, you care about her pain. Remember how much God loves you – thank Him for His love!

Knowing God by
Being Thankful

Let your lives be built on Him. Then you will overflow with thankfulness.

✳ COLOSSIANS 2:7

Overflows are seldom good. A glass overflows when you pour too much in it. A sink overflows if you leave the water running too long. A tub overflows when the drain is plugged up. Overflows often cause messes.

This Scripture verse is talking about a good overflow, which is when you get so filled up with all the wonderful, amazing things God has done for you that the thankfulness just flows over and runs into all parts of your life! That overflow doesn't make a mess, it brings good things!

ChallengePoint

Have you ever felt so blown away by God's awesome, wonderful, giving love that you can't even find words to express it? Think about all He does for you right now – and let the thanksgiving flow!

About the Author

Carolyn Larsen is an author, actress and experienced speaker with a God-given passion for ministering to women. She has spoken at conferences and retreats around the United States, Canada and India. She also enjoys performing with a local theater troupe as well as with her own ministry team, Flashpoints.

She is a best-selling author with more than 40 books in print for children and adults. Some of her titles include *The Little Girls Bible Storybook*, *The Little Boys Bible Storybook* and *One-Minute Devotions for Girls*. Carolyn lives in Glen Ellyn, IL with her husband of nearly 28 years. She has three children.

One-Minute Devotions for Girls

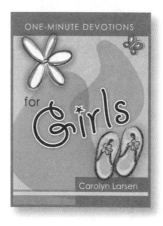

978-1-86920-677-2

A fun and funky one-minute devotional for girls with 366 short readings on a variety of topics concerning their daily walk with God.